THE REPUBLIC OF CTHULHU

Before you start to read this book, take this moment to think about making a donation to punctum books, an independent non-profit press,

@ https://punctumbooks.com/support/

If you're reading the e-book, you can click on the image below to go directly to our donations site. Any amount, no matter the size, is appreciated and will help us to keep our ship of fools afloat. Contributions from dedicated readers will also help us to keep our commons open and to cultivate new work that can't find a welcoming port elsewhere. Our adventure is not possible without your support.
Vive la open-access.

Fig. 1. Hieronymus Bosch, *Ship of Fools* (1490–1500)

THE REPUBLIC OF CTHULHU: LOVECRAFT, THE WEIRD TALE, AND CONSPIRACY THEORY Copyright © 2016 Eric Wilson. This work carries a Creative Commons BY-NC-SA 4.0 International license, which means that you are free to copy and redistribute the material in any medium or format, and you may also remix, transform, and build upon the material, as long as you clearly attribute the work to the authors and editors (but not in a way that suggests the authors or punctum books endorses you and your work), you do not use this work for commercial gain in any form whatsoever, and that for any remixing and transformation, you distribute your rebuild under the same license. http://creativecommons.org/licenses/by-nc-sa/4.0/

First published in 2016 by punctum books, Earth, Milky Way.
https://punctumbooks.com

ISBN-13: 978-0-9982375-6-5
ISBN-10: 0-9982375-6-6
Library of Congress Cataloging Data is available from the Library of Congress

Book design: Vincent W.J. van Gerven Oei

The Republic of Cthulhu

Lovecraft, The Weird Tale,
and Conspiracy Theory

by
ERIC WILSON

*This book is dedicated to the memory of my grandparents,
Walter James Wilson, and Mildred Wilson*

There is a strange urge in my mind: I would like to stop behaving as if I am a rat pressing levers — even if I had to give up the cheese and go hungry for a while. I would like to step outside the conditioning maze and see what makes it tick. I wonder what I would find. Perhaps a terrible superhuman monstrosity the very contemplation of which would make a person insane? Perhaps a solemn gathering of sages? Or the maddening simplicity of unattended clockwork?
— Jacques Vallee

We are property.
— Charles Fort

Acknowledgments

The author would like to thank S.T. Joshi for his generous donation of time in reading and commenting upon an earlier version of this essay. He also extends a very heartfelt "Thank you" to both Eileen Joy and Vincent W.J. van Gerven Oei of punctum books for their exceptional work in bringing this text to completion.

Contents

1
Gods and Monsters | 15

2
The Criminology of the Nameless:
Parapolitics and *Alētheia* | 27

3
From the Sublime:
"The Call of Cthulhu" (1926) | 47

4
To the Grotesque:
"The Horror at Red Hook" (1925) | 89

5
N. Lat. 40.7117°, W. Long. 74.0125°
08:46–09:03 AM, September 11, 2001 | 119

Conclusion:
The Doom that Came to Humanism | 143

Bibliography | 173

1. *Gods and Monsters*

> In art there is no use in heeding the chaos of the universe; for so complete is this chaos, that no piece writ in words could even so much as hint at it. I can conceive of no true image of the pattern of life and cosmic force, unless it be a jumble of mean dots arranged in directionless spirals.
> — H.P. Lovecraft

Weirdly enough, there is no love in H.P. Lovecraft.

> All my stories are based on the fundamental premise that common human laws and interests and emotions have no validity or significance in the vast cosmos-at-large. […] To achieve the essence of real externality, whether of time or space or dimension, one must forget that such things as good and evil, love and hate, and all such local attributes of a negligible and temporary race called mankind, have any existence at all.[1]

Although Lovecraft on numerous occasions referred to his signature literary conceit as "cosmic indifferentism,"[2] the contemporary reader immediately recognizes this trope for what

---

1 Levy, *Lovecraft*, 81.
2 There is some debate over this term. According to S.T. Joshi, Lovecraft may not have ever employed the term "cosmic indifferentism," but merely "indifferentism." Within the secondary literature, however, the term "cosmic disinterestism" is fairy widespread; see below. Joshi, p.c.

is really is: the *un-human*.³ "The Lovecraftian world cannot be changed or controlled. It is a no-man's-land in its arid desolation, without love or warmth. It contains no human value or worth since it does not allow anyone to be represented as the immanent 'I.'"⁴ And in this Universe devoid of an ontologically grounded human "Subject" we are the collective victims of cosmic *disinterestism,* a purely neutral observation on the part of Lovecraft, "a clinical assessment of the human condition that is simple in its fundamental meaning but difficult enough to truly comprehend that a new kind of writing must be invented for the purpose of its telling."⁵ The paradox at work here is obvious: how — or even why — can an artist give expression to a view of the cosmos that is essentially antithetical to the Being-Human-within-the-World? Or, to re-frame the issue in terms of authorial voice: why did Lovecraft, with extreme eccentricity, choose supernatural literature as the aesthetic vehicle for expressing his annihilating nihilism, given that he did, for whatever reason, decide to express it? And it is Lovecraft himself, a "Literary Copernicus" in the words of Fritz Leiber, who provides the answer: "I do not think that any realism is beautiful."⁶

> Individuals and their fortunes within natural law move me very little. They are all momentary trifles bound from a common nothingness toward another common nothingness. Only the cosmic framework itself — or such individuals as symbolize principles (or defiances of principles) of the cosmic framework — can gain a deep grip on my imagination and set it to work creating. In other words, the only "heroes" I can write about are phenomena.⁷

---

3   Thacker, *In the Dust of This Planet*, 1–9.
4   Airaksinen, *The Philosophy of H.P. Lovecraft*, 24. "Lovecraft is a postmodern writer who saw through the existential defense mechanisms of the modern person." Ibid., 183. See below.
5   Martin, *H.P. Lovecraft*, 16.
6   Houellebecq, *H.P. Lovecraft*, 4.
7   Joshi, "Introduction," xv.

S.T. Joshi has articulated Lovecraft's tortuous relation to the literary tropes of realism quite well: "[R]ealism is [...] not a goal but a function in Lovecraft; it facilitates the perception that 'something which could not possibly happen' is actually happening."[8] Personally, I would describe the resultant Lovecraftian landscape as "Miltonian surrealism," the catastrophic collapse of categories of meaning occasioned by the falling to Earth of a supersensible but inhuman reality, Luciferian in its magnificence but "daemonic" in its effects. In any event, Lovecraft's ceaseless parodying of "the Real" constitutes the idiosyncratic expression of the author's commitment to that nebulous sub-genre known as cosmic horror. Although apparently linked to the supernatural theme in literature, Lovecraft's oeuvre, on closer examination, reveals a meta-narrative that is thoroughly "mainstream" modernist in orientation. And this supernaturally-infused modernism, in turn, betrays an almost nostalgic invocation of the notions of both numinousity and transcendence, an atheistic interrogation and re-conceptualization of "the Holy" that is a central but largely underappreciated facet of the literary project of modernism. In truth, the seminal text on the subject of horrific transcendence, Rudolf Otto's *The Idea of the Holy* (1917), reads suspiciously like a compendium of Lovecraftian narrative devices. Operating from a Wittgensteinian premise — "An object that can thus be thought conceptually may be termed *rational*" — Otto turns dogmatic theology on its head by arguing for the opposite axiom: any object that maybe considered real (as in possessing substance) yet lacking "clear and definite concepts" must necessarily be considered irrational; that is, an existent that is shapeless or formless.[9] In theological terms, this antiformalist insight yields us the category of the numinous which, in existential terms, is subjectively experienced as the "Holy" or the *mysterium tremendum,* the phenomenological core of Religion.[10] A union of light and dark — *mysterium* as a kind of fasci-

---

8 Cited in MacCormack, "Lovecraft through Deleuzio-Guattarian Gates," 1.
9 Otto, *The Idea of the Holy,* 1.
10 Ibid., 12–13.

nation[11] and *tremendum* as a source of dread[12] — Otto breaks the "daunting" latter aspect of the Holy down into three overlapping components. The first is "awe-fulness" or "daemonical dread," the spectral fear induced by the direct and unmediated encounter with an undefinable and hitherto invisible "Wholly Other."[13]

> It first begins to stir in the feeling of "something uncanny," "eerie," or "weird." It is this feeling which, emerging in the mind of primeval man, forms the starting-point for the entire religious development of history. "Daemons" and "gods" alike spring from this root, and all the products of "mythological apperception" or "fantasy" are nothing but different modes in which it has been objectified.[14]

The second is alternatively defined as "energy" or "urgency," the raw power of psychic transformation and an annihilating, de-personalizing illumination.[15] Like awefulness, energy is both primitive and visceral, best expressed within the Abrahamic tradition as "the scorching and consuming wrath of God,"[16] a reservoir of supernatural energy that appears devoid of moral qualities; "It is [...] 'like a hidden force of nature,' like stored-up electricity, discharging itself upon anyone who comes too near. It is 'incalculable' and 'arbitrary.'"[17] Significantly, in its "positive" form, it manifests itself as mystic rapture, "the same 'energy'" as "the scorching and consuming wrath of God" but flowing through different channels ("'Love,' says one of the mystics, 'is nothing else than quenched wrath.'"[18]) The third, and the one

---

11 Ibid., 25–40. The signature emotion of *mysterium* is *stupor,* "an astonishment that strikes us dumb, amazement absolute." Ibid., 26.
12 Ibid., 12–24.
13 Ibid., 13–19 and 25–30.
14 Ibid., 14–15.
15 Ibid., 23–24.
16 Ibid., 24.
17 Ibid., 18. In the words of the analytic philosopher Noel Carroll, "Otto's numen [...] defies the application of predicates and even the manifold of predictability itself." Carroll, *The Philosophy of Horror,* 166.
18 Otto, *The Idea of the Holy,* 24.

closest to Lovecraft's own dramatic concerns, is *majestas,* "absolute over-poweringness," or, even better, "creature-consciousness": the "shadow or subjective reflection" of the Self's abject dependency upon the Wholly Other.[19]

> It is the emotion of a creature, submerged and overwhelmed, by its own nothingness in contrast to that which is supreme above all creatures. […] [T]hus, in contrast to "the overpowering" of which we are conscious as an object over against the self, there is the feeling of one's own submergence, of being but "dust and ashes" and nothingness. And this forms the numinous raw material for the feeling of religious humility.[20]

The "I am naught, Thou art all" is the unique and irreducible core of authentic private religious experience in which the "*self-depreciation*" of that primordial "element of the *tremendum,* originally apprehended as 'plenitude of power,' becomes transmuted into 'plenitude of being.'"[21] Or, to put it another way: personal religious experience is the phenomenological mapping of the anthropological migration from Monsters to Gods. If the numinous truly stands for that "aspect of deity which transcends or eludes comprehension in rational or ethical terms,"[22] then Otto's great work makes intelligible one of the most repressed truths of the Sacred: that the inseparability of religion from horror flows from the primordial "absence of difference" between the Wholly Other and the Monster. Derived from the Latin noun *monstrum,* which is related to the verbs *monstrare* ("to show" or "to reveal") and *monere* ("to warn" or "to portend"[23]), the coming of

19 Ibid., 219–23.
20 Ibid., 10 and 20.
21 Ibid., 21.
22 Harvey, in Otto, *The Idea of the Holy,* xvi. See also A.S. Herbert, cited in Cardin, *Dark Awakenings,* 302: "The word 'holy' is primarily not an ethical term, but one indicating the otherness, the incalculable power, of God, his inaccessibility. He is 'the great stranger in the human world' […]. Holy expressed the mysterious, incalculable, unapproachable quality of the divine in contrast to the human."
23 Beal, *Religion and Its Monsters,* 6–7.

the Monster is identical to a revelation of a dangerous truth that is incommensurable with orthodox consensus, both social and epistemological. In its existential dimension, the numinous/monstrous is identical with that unsayable-which-induces-dread and which, therefore, lacks a true name; the "nearest that German can get to it is in the expression *das Ungeheuere* (monstrous), while in English 'weird' is perhaps the closest rendering possible."[24] In its anthropological dimension, God-and-Monster signifies both the iterability between Chaos and Order (the eternally recurrent migrations between cosmogony and chaogony) as well as the radically undecidable (anti-schematic) nature of the primal substance of Being.[25] At the risk of simplifying, it may be said that the greater part of the intellectual edifice of Lovecraft's oeuvre consists of nothing more than an act of translation of what Beal identifies as "the paradox of the monstrous"[26] into the atheistic tropes of Darwinian biology and Einsteinian physics. What he yields is an utterly "uncanny" synthesis of the archaic with the super scientific, a monstrous cross-fertilization of the transcendental Wholly Other with the materialist Alien.

> Paradoxically, it is precisely this bleak atheist awe that makes Lovecraft a kind of bad-son heir to a religious visionary tradition, an ecstatic tradition, which, in distinction to the everyday separation of matter and spirit, locates the holy in the everyday. Lovecraft, too, sees the awesome as immanent in the quotidian, but there is little ecstasy [*mysterium*] here: his is a bad numinous.[27]

---

24 Otto, *The Idea of the Holy*, 40.
25 See Beal, *Religion and Its Monsters*. Also see Cardin, "A Horrific Reading of Isaiah," in Cardin, *Dark Awakenings*, 287–319. Cardin ends his discussion of the Book of Isaiah 24–34 by concluding "Yahweh, in a very important way, functions as a chaos monster." Ibid., 295; also, 296, 300, and 302.
26 Beal, *Religion and Its Monsters*, 19.
27 Joshi, "Introduction," xiii. Compare Ralickas on this very point: "In denying humanism and revealing the ostensible unity of the human subject to be a fallacy, I contend that what Lovecraft's work affirms, albeit negatively, is a subjective crisis specific to the modern condition." Ralickas, "Cosmic Horror," 366; see also ibid., 387–88.

Following Otto, we can now see that the central conceit of the Lovecraftian corpus is that his "bad numinous" is *tremendum* with the *mysterium* subtracted out (although it should be noted that Lovecraft does seek a limited re-introduction of "fascination" or stupor in relation to the Wholly Other in some of his last works[28]). Lovecraft himself makes this painfully clear in his semi-confessional work of literary criticism "Supernatural Horror in Literature" (1927).

> The appeal of the spectrally macabre is generally narrow because it demands from the reader a certain degree of imagination and a capacity of detachment from everyday life. [...] There is here involved a psychological pattern or tradition as real and as deeply grounded in mental experience as any other pattern or tradition of mankind; coeval with the religious feeling and closely related to many aspects of it, and too much a part of our inmost biological heritage to lose keen potency over a very important, though not numerically great, minority of our species.[29]

Typically, Lovecraft grounds the species's predilection for horror with an atavistic genetic inheritance.[30] "The oldest and strongest emotion of mankind is fear, and the oldest and strongest kind of fear is fear of the unknown." The artistic merit of "the weirdly horrible tale as a literary form," therefore, is guaranteed not by transcendental notions but by profanely material ones: the literary re-enactment of the primal terror of self-awareness.[31]

---

28 In particular, "At the Mountains of Madness" and "The Shadow over Innsmouth." See Chapter Five, below.

29 Lovecraft, "Supernatural," 105.

30 As does Otto. "It may well be possible, it is even probable, that in the first stage of its development the religious consciousness started with only one of its poles — the daunting aspect of the numen — and so at first took shape only as 'daemonic dread.'" Otto, *The Idea of the Holy*, 32.

31 Lovecraft, "Supernatural," 105. Compare this remarkable passage with Otto on the atavistic relationship between daemonic dread and horror fiction: "This crudely naïve and primordial emotional disturbance, and the fantastic images to which it gives rise, are later overborne and ousted by more

Against the emotional primacy of horror "are discharged all the shafts of a materialistic sophistication which clings to frequently felt emotions and external events, and of a naively insipid idealism which deprecates the aesthetic motive and calls for a didactic literature to 'uplift' the reader towards a suitable degree of smirking optimism."[32] However, since cosmic horror is the re-visitation of the (un-)holy, it necessarily follows that the highest form of supernatural literature, or "the weird tale," will necessarily depend upon the successful narrative deployment of the cultural residue of the theological imaginary.

> The true weird tale has something more than secret murder, bloody bones, or a sheeted form clanking chains according to a rule. A certain atmosphere of breathless and unexplainable dread of outer, unknown forces must be present; and there must be a hint, expressed with a seriousness and portentousness becoming its subject, of that most terrible conception of the human brain — a malign and particular suspension or defeat of those fixed laws of Nature which are our only safeguard against the assaults of chaos and the daemons of unplumbed space.[33]

As Lovecraft's greatest critic Maurice Levy points out, the overriding aesthetic impulse of the Lovecraftian text is to induce

> highly developed forms of the numinous emotion, with all its mysteriously impelling power. But even when this has long attained its higher and purer mode of expression it is possible for the primitive types of excitation that were formerly a part of it to break out in the soul in all their original naiveté and so to be experienced afresh. That this is so is shown by the potent attraction again and again exercised by the element of horror and 'shudder' in ghost stories, even among persons of high all-round education." Otto, *The Idea of the Holy*, 16. See also ibid., 29, where Otto clearly identifies "the fear of ghosts" as a "degraded offshoot and travesty of the genuine 'numinous' dread or awe." As Stephen King expressed it, in his inestimable EC horror comic book style, horror "invites a physical reaction by showing us something which [that?] is physically wrong." King, *Danse Macabre*, 22.

32 Lovecraft, "Supernatural," 105.
33 Ibid., 107.

within the post-theistic reader a sense of that primordial dread that was the hallmark of primitive religious experience, the violent and unmediated encounter with the Wholly Other.[34]

> Therefore we must judge a weird tale not by the author's intent, or by the mere mechanics of the plot; but by the emotional level which it attains at its least mundane point. [...] The one test of the really weird is simply this — whether or not there be excited in the reader a profound sense of dread, and of contact with unknown spheres and powers; a subtle attitude of awed listening, as if for the beating of black wings or the scratching of outside shapes and entities on the known universe's utmost rim.[35]

Cosmic horror is a paradoxically anti-therapeutical form of catharsis: curative because of the flooding release of psychic tension that it itself creates, but harmful at the same time because of the radical disabuse of human conceit that it involves. As Donald R. Burleson has quite correctly recognized, Lovecraft's aesthetic is essentially post-modern in nature, a "deconstructive gesture of questioning and unsettling metaphysically privileged systems of all kinds." The signature feature of Lovecraft's writing is precisely this "ironically self-understood insignificance" of Being-Human, which, given the essentially anthropocentric nature of Western thought, bestows upon the Lovecraftian corpus a status unique within modern literature.[36] "In a society that is becoming each day more and more anesthetized and repressive, the fantastic is at once an evasion and the mobilization of anguish. It restores man's sense of the sacred and the sacrilegious, it above all gives back to him his lost depth."[37] For Levy,

---

34 Levy, *Lovecraft*.
35 Lovecraft, "Supernatural," 108.
36 Burleson, *Lovecraft*, 158–59.
37 Levy, *Lovecraft*, 120.

> Lovecraft [...] creates the strange, he excites fear, by *turning the world inside out*. For Lovecraft, writing is making of the oneiric and wrong side of things appear, substituting the nocturnal for the diurnal, replacing the reassuring image of the Waking World by the alienating ones of the great depths. The world of the surface has in his work no other raison d'etre than provisionally and imperfectly to cover up the abyss.[38]

Central to Lovecraft's oeuvre is his highly aestheticized — which is to say, intensely singular — onto-epistemology, a philosophically naïve but dramatically powerful re-presentation of the metaphysics of Schopenhauer[39]; "Life is a hideous thing, and from the background behind what we know of it peer daemonical hints of truth which make it a thousand-fold more hideous."[40] In his pioneering deconstruction of the Lovecraftian weird tale, Burleson identifies as the meta-theme of the oeuvre "the ruinous nature of self-knowledge," or, more exactly, "the notion that, when we as humans come to look upon the cosmos as it is, we find our place in it to be soul-crushingly evanescent."[41] The other recursive themes are "forbidden knowledge," "denied primacy," "unwholesome survivals," and, most interesting of all, "illusory surface appearances," the general signification that "things are not as they appear on the surface, below which deeper and more terrible realities are masked." All of Lovecraft's plots (insofar as there are any) are occasioned by a traumatic, and traumatizing, cognitive rupturing of the social consensus of reality,[42] culminating in the annihilating revelation of an unspeakable dis-joint between human(-istic) phenomena and un-human(-istic) noumena, perfectly suited to the post-theistic aesthetic experience

---

38 Ibid.
39 See below, Chapter Five.
40 Lovecraft, "Facts," 14.
41 Burleson, *Lovecraft*, 158; see ibid., 156–57.
42 "At some point, the text breaks down and reveals something which has not been there. A rupture emerges and, along with it, something new, the unknown. The next step is horror which arises from a threat, not to the narrator but to humanity." Airaksinen, *The Philosophy of H.P. Lovecraft*, 175.

of the weird tale, signified by the obliteration of consciousness and self-awareness, culminating in Lovecraft's trademark literary gimmick: the primordial *scream*. This scream is the epitome of the Lovecraftian artistic effect: a radically alienating encounter with the annihilating — or, in Lovecraft's own terminology, the "brain-blasting"[43] — nature of the Universe, which in the final instance can only be denoted as *the nameless*.

But, by a happy(?) coincidence, "the nameless" is exactly the term that I would use to denote the parapolitical.

---

43 To provide just one typical example: "As I shivered and brooded on the casting of that brain-blasting shadow, I knew that I had pried out one of the earth's supreme horrors — one of those nameless blights of outer voids whose faint demon scratchings we sometimes hear on the furthest rim of space, yet from which our own finite vision has given us merciful immunity." Lovecraft, "The Lurking Fear," 67.

2. The Criminology of the Nameless: *Parapolitics and* Alētheia

> CAMILLA: You, sir, should unmask.
> STRANGER: Indeed?
> CASSILDA: Indeed, it's time.
> We have all laid aside disguise but you.
> STRANGER: I wear no mask.
> CAMILLA: (*Terrified, aside to Cassilda*) No mask? No mask!
> THE KING IN YELLOW: Act I–Scene 2d.
> — Robert W. Chambers, "The Mask"

Parapolitics, the branch of radical criminology that treats the domain of the extra-judicially "weird," bears an uncanny (*unheimlich*) resemblance to the Lovecraftian notion of horror and its attendant fatal de-centering of the rational subject. The irreducible multiplicity of the extra-judicial affinities between clandestine agency and public order thoroughly subvert mainstream criminology's current preoccupation with models of good governance, transparency, and rule-compliance as benchmarks of social and political normality[1]; it therefore supersedes the cognitive apparatuses of orthodox social science. The radical crimi-

1   "The tendency of orthodox criminology to focus on private crimes of greed, lust and rage — perhaps we should think of this as criminology's version of the 'nuts, sluts and perverts' fetish that has impoverished the sociology of deviance — has rendered institutional crimes of power, that is, corporate, political and state crimes — relatively minor areas of study within criminology." Michalowski, "Power, Crime and Criminology," 312.

27

nological term for this hitherto "nameless condition" is *criminal sovereignty* — "the historical moment by which we happen to be governed" — and has been most thoroughly defined by Robert Cribb as the study of "criminals behaving as sovereigns and sovereigns behaving as criminals in a systematic way"; the task, therefore, of parapolitics as a discipline is "to identify the dynamics of that relationship and to delimit precisely the influence that it has, or does not have, on public politics."[2] For Cribb, criminal sovereignty and the clandestine (anti-)truth of the (para-)state is

> not just a topic but an analytical conclusion. On the one hand, it goes significantly beyond the proposition that relations between security and intelligence organisations, international criminal networks and quasi-states are occasional and incidental, the work of "rogue elements" and the like. On the other hand, it falls significantly short of grand conspiracy theory: it does not suggest that the world of visible, "normal" politics is an illusion or that it is entirely subordinated to "deep" politics. Rather, it proposes that the tripartite relationship between security and intelligence organisations, international criminal networks and quasi-states is systematic, extensive and influential.[3]

As I have argued elsewhere,[4] any state that has been (extra-)constitutionally reconstituted under the aegis of criminal sovereignty (or, in the alternative, has been politically and economically reduced to the pure functionality of the ideological mystification of liberalism and democratic consensus) may be expected to exhibit the following four signs: *governance* as a substitute for government (the collapse of the distinction between "public state" and "civil society," resulting in an open-ended but clandestine "privatization" of the state); *duality* (the

---

2 Cribb, "Introduction," 8.
3 Ibid.
4 See Wilson, *Government of the Shadows* and Wilson, *The Dual State*.

iterable relationship between what is conventionally denoted as both "law" and "crime"); *nomadicism* (a chaotic proliferation of supra-statist, statist, and sub-statist entities, all of an indeterminate, or liminal, juridical nature, that regularly transverse established juro-political boundaries[5]); and the *irrational* (the invisible co-option of the "public interest" by the "private actor").

Given that the true discursive object of parapolitics is the inherently "nameless" — the fatally anti-liberal substance of criminal sovereignty — I have come to appreciate the need for radical criminology to engage with language and literary expression in a far more self-reflective manner than has previously been the case. The successful performance of parapolitical analysis as suggested by Cribb ultimately rests upon its ability to radically re-conceptualize the myriad relationships among public identity and clandestine agency. In order to be wholly successful within its own research matrix, therefore, parapolitics requires its own and singular form of discourse, or, even more precisely, poetics. As the cliched purpose of art is to express the otherwise inexpressible, aesthetics provides the necessary supplement to conventional social theory to convey a sense of the "weirdness" of parapolitical phenomena — or, more exactly, its forbidden or *ineffable* substance. Aesthetics, or *aisthētikos* in its Hellenic form, denotes "perceptive by feeling"; its domain is not art(-ifice) but visceral Reality, "corporeal, material nature," a "form of cognition, achieved through taste, touch, hearing, seeing, smell — the whole corporeal sensorium [...]."[6] Since aesthetics, as Terry Eagleton holds, "is born as a discourse of the body,"[7] it cannot be subject to direct or immediate verbalization, but can only be understood, if at all, on the level of the intuitive (naïve) or the

---

5 Here, I am employing "nomadicism" in the sense of "the nomadic" as developed by Deleuze and Guattari, *A Thousand Plateaus*, 351–423. The nomadic denotes not only a free-moving material agent or agency but also the ontological indeterminacy of the nomadic force itself, the crypto-materialist equivalent of the "un-decidable" in deconstruction. For further elaboration, see below.

6 Buck-Morss, "Aesthetics and Anaesthetics," 6.

7 Eagleton, *The Ideology of the Aesthetic*, 13.

phenomenological (sophisticated). Here, the classical aesthetic theory of the eighteenth century, which exhibited a profound concern with the somatic vitality of the beautiful, may come in handy. In Part One of a *Philosophical Enquiry into the Origin of Ideas of the Sublime and Beautiful* (1757), Edmund Burke makes a series of interesting observations about "obscurity."[8] A synonym for the ineffable, obscurity, or, more precisely, the obscure is that thing which is present but yet cannot be directly perceived nor clearly described; that which is obscure is that to which no clearly discernible outline, or borders, can be assigned. And this leads directly into a consideration of the aesthetic significance of magnitude, or infinity.

> But let it be considered that hardly anything can strike the mind with its greatness, which does not make some sort of approach towards infinity; which nothing can do whilst we are able to perceive its bounds; but to see an object distinctly, and to perceive its bounds, is one and the same thing. A clear idea is therefore another name for a little idea.[9]

Obscurity is directly linked by association to fear, or terror, which also turns on the absence of clear sight: "[N]ight increases our terror perhaps more than anything else; it is our nature that when we do not know what may happen to us, to fear the worst that can happen to us; and hence it is that uncertainty is so terrible, that we often seek to be rid of it, at the hazard of a certain mischief."[10] Both obscurity and, most especially, terror,

---

8   Burke, *A Philosophical Enquiry*, 99–100.
9   Ibid., 107–8. An observation that Lovecraft apparently intuited while still in near infancy: "What has haunted my dreams for nearly forty years is *a strange sense of adventurous expectancy connected with landscape and architecture and sky-effects*. I can see myself as a child of 2 and one half years on the railway bridge at Auburndale, Mass., looking across and downward at the business parts of town, and feeling the imminence of some wonder which I could neither describe nor fully conceive." Lovecraft, "The Case of Charles Dexter Ward," 392, fn. 15. Emphasis in the original.
10 Ibid., 153–54. It is tempting to identify this "certain mischief" with conspiracy theory.

are two of the signifiers of the archetypal aesthetic phenomenon that is the true focus of Burke's concern, the *sublime*: "[W]ithout a strong impression nothing can be sublime."[11] Derived from the Latin *sublimis* (elevated; lofty), the sublime is directly suggestive of two more subversive concepts, *limen* (the threshold) and *limes* (border; boundary; limit),[12] both of which connote liminality, which I have already identified as a principal sign of the parapolitical.

> Whatever is fitted in any sort to excite the ideas of pain, and danger, that is to say, whatever is in any sort terrible, or is conversant about terrible objects, or operates in a manner analogous to terror, is a source of the *sublime*; that is, it is productive of the strongest emotion which the mind is capable of feeling.[13]

A psychological hedonist, Burke's taxonomy of sentiment is strictly binary, the two most powerful emotions being pleasure and pain.[14] Pleasure encompasses beauty while pain encompasses terror, dread, and fear, which receive their aesthetic correlation in the sublime:

> The passions which belong to self-preservation, turn on pain and danger; they are simply painful when their causes immediately affect us; they are delightful [productive of a sense of relief, when one has been safely immured from the dangerous object[15]] when we have an idea of pain and danger, without actually being in such circumstances; this delight I have not called pleasure [binary logic], because it turns on pain, and because it is different enough from any idea of positive pleasure. Whatever excites this delight, I call *sublime*. The

11 Ibid., 144.
12 S. Morley, "Introduction," 14.
13 Burke, *A Philosophical Enquiry,* 58–59.
14 Ibid., 43–58.
15 Ibid., 52.

> passions belonging to self-preservation [the flight from pain, danger and death[16]] are the strongest of all passions.[17]

Although clearly linked with the obscure, terror, for Burke, is the true harbinger of the approach of the sublime: "No passion so effectually robs the mind of all its powers of acting and reasoning as fear. For fear, being an apprehension of pain or death [...] operates in a manner that resembles actual [rather than merely imagined] pain."[18] Terror, as the root cause of the sublime ("A mode of terror, or of pain, is always the cause of the sublime"[19]) is a form of pain that operates on both the body and the mind ("we have all along considered the sublime as depending on some modification of pain or terror"[20]), constituting a second binary relationship paralleling that of pain/pleasure; what impresses the contemporary reader most is Burke's emphatically somatic concept of both terror and the sublime.

> Fear or terror [...] is an appreciation of pain or death. [...] The only difference between pain and terror is that things which cause pain operate on the mind, by the intervention of the body; whereas things that cause terror generally affect the bodily organs by the operation of the mind suggesting the danger.[21] [...] [T]he instances we have given of it [...] relate to such things as are fitted by nature to produce this sort of tension, either by the primary operation of the mind or the body.[22]

Therefore, the sublime possesses a wide variety of attributes dispersed throughout the natural world which act as objective

16 Ibid., 57–58.
17 Ibid., 84–85.
18 Ibid., 96.
19 Ibid., 258.
20 Ibid., 273.
21 Ibid., 247–48.
22 Ibid., 252–53.

causes of terror[23]: Power ("I know of nothing sublime which is not some modification of power"[24]); privation; vastness; infinity; succession and uniformity (via the infinite multiplication of visual landscapes[25]); magnitude in building/architecture; infinity in pleasing objects; difficulty; magnificence; light; light in buildings; color; sound and loudness; suddenness; intermitting of sound; the cries of animals; smell and taste: bitters and stenches ("I shall only observe that no smell or tastes can produce a grand sensation, except excessive bitters and intolerable stenches"[26]); feeling pain[27]; and both darkness and blackness.[28] All four attributes of the parapolitical substance are appropriate subjects of literary appropriation as the sublime — the nomadic, the private, and governance all bespeak of a clandestine "form" that is obscure and, therefore, without clear and discernible limits. To

23 This list bespeaks of an unconscious effort by Burke to conflate the sublime with the theatrical, a point not lost on Jean-Francois Lyotard: "For Burke, the sublime was no longer a matter of elevation (the category by which Aristotle defined tragedy), but a matter of intensification. [...] [A]t the dawn of romanticism, Burke's elaboration of the aesthetics of the sublime [...] outlined a world of possibilities for artistic experiments in which the avant-gardes would later trace out their paths." And avant-gardism is nothing if not pure theatricality. Lyotard, "The Sublime and the Avant-Garde," 35 and 36. Horror as a Burkean somatic/sensory experience is the central thesis of Ndalianis; see generally. Dr. Marnius Bicknell Willet's katabatic peregrinations through the cyclopean catacombs that take up the whole of the penultimate section of Lovecraft's "The Case of Charles Dexter Ward," is a veritable encyclopaedia of the Burkean signs of the sublime. Lovecraft, "The Case of Charles Dexter Ward," 175–90.
24 Burke, *A Philosophical Enquiry*, 110.
25 Ibid., 268–72.
26 Ibid., 156. An observation certainly not lost upon Lovecraft; no other writer of horror relied so heavily upon an annihilating stench to convey the sense of the sublime Other. Take, for example, this passage from the seminal weird tale "The Call of Cthulhu": "There was a bursting as of an exploding bladder, a slushy nastiness as of a cloven sunfish, a stench as of a thousand opened graves, and a sound that the chronicler could not put on paper. For an instant the ship was befouled by an acrid and blinding green cloud, and then there was only a venomous seething astern." Lovecraft, "The Call of Cthulhu," 156. See below.
27 Ibid., 110–60.
28 Ibid., 272–86.

take a pedestrian example: the irrefutable proof of the existence of a second gunman on the grassy knoll in Dallas who is also an enforcer for the Corsican mafia under contract to the anti-Castro Cuban leadership acting in an informal alliance with rogue elements within the CIA for the purposes of subverting John F. Kennedy's informal overtures of détente with the Soviet Union would cause the impartial observer to seriously question the solidity of the boundaries demarcating the public government of the U.S. from the "shadow" State[29] of the national intelligence agencies — in other words, the revelation of such a truth would cause the sentiment of fear (and possibly its social equivalent, moral panic). When exposed to conspiratorial reality the naif has no response available to her other than the truism "No one is safe," which is nothing other than the inversion of the dark adage "Trust no one," suggesting an *infinite* array of potential suspects. For Burke, as for the newcomer to conspiracy theory, the more accurate term to give to the subjective feeling of this sudden and unexpected apperception of the sublime would be *astonishment*.

> [A]stonishment is that state of the soul in which all its motions are suspended, with some degree of horror. In this case the mind is so entirely filled with its object that it cannot entertain any other, nor, by consequences, reason on that object which employs it. Hence arises the great power of the sublime, that far from being produced by them it anticipates our reasonings and hurries us on by an irresistible force. Aston-

---

29 A quintessentially Burkean notion, as "shadow" denotes the darkness, a universal causation of that terror which is the sublime: "[A]n association which takes in all of mankind may make darkness terrible; for in utter darkness it is impossible to know in what degree of safety we stand; we are ignorant of the objects that surround us; we may every moment strike against some dangerous obstruction; we may fall down a precipice the first step we take; and if an enemy approach, we know not in what quarter to defend ourselves; in such a case strength is of no sure protection; wisdom can only act by guess; the boldest are staggered, and he who would pray for nothing else towards his defense is forced to pray for light." Ibid., 273–74.

ishment [...] is the effect of the sublime in its highest degree; the inferior effects are admiration, reverence and respect.[30]

However, I argue that it is only the fourth attribute — the irrational — that constitutes a proper and formal artistic phenomenon in its own right, due to its deeply meaningful but highly problematic relevance to the classical aesthetic categories of both the sublime and its diminutive twin, the grotesque.[31] If I were to provide a list of possible authors that could serve as useful literary exemplars for the aesthetically "knowing" parapolitical scholar, it would include "subversive" writers as diverse as Jorge Luis Borges, Leonardo Sciascia, Alain Robbe-Grillet, Don DeLillo, Thomas Pynchon, William Burroughs, Denis Johnson, Don Winslow, J.G. Ballard, Edogawa Rampo, James Ellroy, and Reza Negarestani. But at the very top of that list would stand H.P. Lovecraft: the "natural" literary trope for an aestheticized form of parapolitical discourse is cosmic horror and the weird tale. As Graham Harman has proven, it is the unmediated encounter with the ineffable that serves as the basis of Lovecraft's inimitable style: the strategic deployment of the *oblique* manifested through a symphonic accumulation of allusions that effects the wholesale separation of the individual (and individualizing) qualities of a thing from that thing, which is now rendered as literally unspeakable.[32] Through the judicious deployment of discursive gaps within the (ostensibly) "objective" description of the Wholly Other, Lovecraft, against all odds, is able to convincingly allude to some unidentifiable remnant utterly real and viscerally present that extends beyond the purely empirical account

30 Ibid., 95–96.
31 See below, Chapters Three and Four.
32 Harman, *Weird Realism*, 28–32. Harman denotes this hyper-accumulation of allusions as "literary cubism": "[N]umerous bizarre or troubling features of a palpable thing are piled up in such excessive number that it becomes difficult to combine all these facets into a single object, thereby giving us the sense of a purely immanent object that is nonetheless distinct from any bundle of features." Ibid., 234.

of the thing.[33] Under Lovecraft's hands, the meaning of being is re-presented as *untranslatability*; "Language (and everything else) is obliged to become an art of allusion or indirect speech, a metaphorical bond with a reality that cannot possibly be made present."[34] And this fetish of the oblique is not the adolescent affectation that Lovecraft's critics routinely despise him for: it is objectively impossible to adequately paraphrase an oblique account of an ineffable object, and to do so, as Harman convincingly shows, leads to pure stupidity (as would the reverse; for example: "I constructed for myself that item commonly known as a sandwich, which is a meaty core ensconced by two spongy parallel layers whose chemical composition excluded all vegetable matter other than that of wheat.") An unmediated encounter with the ineffable logically demands an oblique style for reasons both of epistemology and literature. It should come as no surprise, then, that the progressive scholarship of Peter Dale Scott, the parapolitical researcher who most self-consciously strives to formulate a form of poetics through which to convey new understandings of untranslatable political phenomena, lends itself supremely well to a "Lovecraftian" application. Rightly according pre-eminence to the as yet still under-appreciated phenomenon of the politically irrational, Scott defines parapolitics in the following manner.

> 1. A system or practice of politics in which accountability is consciously diminished. 2. Generally, covert politics, the conduct of public affairs not by rational debate and responsible decision-making but by indirection, collusion, and deceit. Cf. *conspiracy*. 3. The political exploitation of irresponsible agencies or para-structures, such as intelligence agencies.[35]

---

[33] "There are many truths and there is one reality, but their relationship must remain oblique rather than direct […]. Lovecraft grasps better than any other writer of fiction […] this notion of a purely oblique access to a genuine reality." Ibid., 262, fn. 15.

[34] Ibid., 16.

[35] Scott, *War Conspiracy*, 238.

For Scott, the essence of the parapolitical is an "intervening layer of irrationality under our political culture's rational surface."[36] The submerged, or repressed, nature of covert agency is not only an ontological problem but an epistemological one as well; it is precisely because of its irrational nature that the parapolitical evades cognitive recognition, with all of the attendant ideological implications, effectively subverting all orthodox liberal understandings of the state.[37]

> Just as politics as a field ("political science") studies the overt politics of the public state, so parapolitics, as a field, studies the relationships between the public state and the political processes and arrangements outside and beyond conventional politics. However, conventional, or liberal, political science assumes the normalcy of the state, both in its constitutional and normative dimensions, as a given and studies political phenomenon from the perspective of the state. Parapolitics, in contrast, constitutes a radically nominalist critique of conventional political studies. Parapolitics uses the varying levels of interaction between conventional states and quasi-statist entities as the basis for formulating an analytical perspective that privileges neither the state nor its alternatives as legitimate international actors. Although of no determinative political bias, parapolitics does foster a basic scepticism regarding the coherence of orthodox liberal understandings of the state.[38]

Precisely because the Real is the irrational, mainstream scholarship is rendered thoroughly oblivious to the operational presence of the parapolitical mechanisms of governance, collectively denoted as the *Deep State*.

---

36 Scott, *Deep Politics and the Death of JFK*, 6–7.
37 Wilson, "Deconstructing the Shadows," 30.
38 Ibid.

> Liberal political science has been turned into an ideology of the "deep state" because undisputable evidence for the [national security] "deep state" is brushed away as pure fantasy or conspiracy[39] [...]. Thus, the problem with liberalism in political science and legal theory is not its ambition to defend the public sphere, political freedoms and human rights, but rather its claim that these freedoms and rights define the Western political system.[40]

Now compare this passage with Lovecraft: "We know things [...] only through our five senses or our religious intuitions: wherefore it is quite impossible to refer to any object or spectacle which cannot be clearly depicted by the solid definitions of fact or the current doctrines of theology."[41]

For Scott, parapolitical scholarship has enabled us to directly perceive two aspects of the Deep State.[42] My own predilection, however, is to resist the totalizing implications of the language of Scott's more recent work; in place of the seemingly monolithic Deep State,[43] I prefer the radically pluralistic (if not latently schizophrenic) notion of Scott's original term, the *Dual State*.

39 Ola Tunander, cited in Wilson, "Deconstructing the Shadows," 29.
40 Tunander, "Democratic State vs. Deep State," 68.
41 Lovecraft, "The Unnamable," 91. One should be careful here not to confuse the voice of a character with the presence of the author; a devout atheist, Lovecraft never would have referred to religion in anything other than a cynical manner — Joshi, p.c. Nevertheless, the crypto-Schopenhauerian notion of a world-order independent of both the senses and received dogma yet real in a super-sensible way is clearly one of Lovecraft's central themes.
42 "The potentially larger condition of a shadow government, or a state within a state, is what we may call the *deep state phenomenon*. But there [is] also the more operational sense of the *deep state connection*: a hard-edged coalition of willing forces including intelligence networks, official enforcement, illegal sanctioned violence, and an internationally connected drug mafia." Scott, *American War Machine*, 21.
43 "Today everything that has ever been labelled 'invisible government,' or 'shadow government' can be considered parts of that machine — not just the CIA and organized crime but also such other non-accountable powers as the military-industrial complex (now the financial-military-industrial complex), privatized military and intelligence contractors, public relations experts, and even Washington's most highly organized lobbyists." Ibid.

> The Dual State. A *State* in which one can distinguish between a *public state* and a top-down *deep state.* The deep state emerges in a false-flag violence, is organized by the military and intelligence apparatus and involves their link to organized crime. Most states exhibit this duality, but to varying degrees. In America the duality of the state has become more and more acute since World War II.[44]

The dual nature, or duality, of the state signifies the suspension of political monism and the division of the residual "state" into a public domain and a (quasi-) private "para-state." Even more subversive is the (potentially) unlimited sub-division of the para-state into multifarious and competing clandestine groupings. The extent of the duality of the state correlates precisely with transversal operations of covert power; the public state that is the phenomenal manifestation of the clandestine noumena suffers an absolute loss of onto-political meaning by that fact alone.

> So it is that thousands of plots in favor of the established order tangle and clash almost everywhere, as the overlap of secret networks and secret issues or activities grows ever more dense along with their rapid integration into every sector of economics, politics and culture. In all areas of social life the degree of intermingling in surveillance, disinformation and security activities gets greater and greater. The plot having thickened to the point where it is almost out in the open, each part of it now starts to interfere with, or worry, the others, for all these professional conspirators are spying on each other without really knowing why, are colliding by chance yet not identifying each other with any certainty [...]. In the

---

44 Scott, *War Conspiracy,* 238. In turn, the "dual state" equates with a "deep political system," which Scott defines as "one which habitually resorts to decision-making and enforcement procedures outside as well as inside those publicly sanctioned by law and society. In popular terms, collusive secrecy and law-breaking are part of how the deep political system works." Scott, *Deep Politics,* xi–xii.

same network and apparently pursuing similar goals, those who are only a part of the network are necessarily ignorant of the hypothesizes and conclusions of the other parts, and above all of their controlling nucleus.[45]

But the truly vital connective thread between Lovecraft and Scott lies within their respective meditations upon the primacy of the "occult" manipulation of public perception and rational speech — "*suitable degree of smirking optimism*" — that is the foundation of the ultimate success of the anti-Human conspiracy of cosmic horror. For Scott, no less than for Lovecraft, a stage-managed form of universal cognitive dissonance constitutes the highest form of parapolitical (or "daemonical"[46]) governance; in Scott's terminology, the mass production and consumption of deep events, "events that are systematically ignored, suppressed, or falsified in public (and even internal) government, military, and intelligence documents as well as in the mainstream media and public consciousness." Like Lovecraft, Scott has conceived of modern civilization as "a great conspiracy of organized denial," the creation of a "partly illusory mental space in which unpleasant facts, such as that all Western empires have been established through major atrocities, are conveniently suppressed."[47] Deploying the deep event as an instrument of parapolitical hermeneutics, Scott has advanced the proposition that the inte-

---

45 Debord, *Comments*, 82–83.
46 Relying upon his formidable knowledge of classical civilization, Lovecraft repeatedly employs the "daemonic," which is a gnostic/theurgic term, instead of the "demonic," which is a Christian/Manichaean term. As Lovecraft is ultimately concerned with issues of cosmic awareness and world-historical systems of institutionalized misperception, the use of the gnostic term may, in fact, be more appropriate here, even if unintentionally so. See Cardin, "A Brief History of the Angel and the Demon," in Cardin, *Dark Awakenings*, 182–240. According to S.T. Joshi, however, Lovecraft's spelling is merely an affected British-ism rather than a trace of a concealed metaphysical belief. — Joshi, p.c. In any event, it is an interesting usage. It is also the one that appears in the English-language translation of Otto's *The Idea of the Holy*, which might provide evidence, albeit weak, that Lovecraft utilized this text as a pseudo-"instruction manual."
47 Scott, *American War Machine*, 3.

grated spectacle is the interpretative key of the national history of the U.S.

> In American history there are two types of events. There are ordinary events which the information systems of the country can understand and transmit. There are also deep events, or mega-events, which the mainstream information systems of the country cannot digest. I mean by a "deep event" one in which it is clear from the outset that there are aspects which will not be dealt with in the mainstream media, and will be studied only by those so-called conspiracy theorists' who specialize in deep history.[48]

Understood not as an accumulation of episodic events but as manifestations of foundational systemic properties, these deep events "suggest the on-going presence in America of what I have called a 'dark force' or 'deep state,' analogous to what [Vicenzo] Vinciguerra described in Italy as a 'secret force [...] occult and hidden, with the capacity of giving a strategic direction to the [successive] outrages.'"[49] For Scott, then, "national security state conspiracies" as deep events serve as "components of our political structure, not deviations from them."[50]

If I were to offer a more sophisticated philosophical analysis of both Scott's and Lovecraft's respective deployments of collective denial as a form of parapolitical/daemonical governance, then an obvious place to begin would be with Martin Heidegger's seminal treatment of the classical Greek notion of *alētheia,* or "revelation." For Heidegger,[51] the inherently political nature of the relationship between the political being of the unified state and political reason (*ratio*) "springs from the essence of truth as correctness in the sense of the self-adjusting guarantee of the security of domination. The 'taking as true' of *ratio,* of

48 Scott, cited in Wilson, *The Spectacle of the False Flag,* 20.
49 Ibid., 21.
50 Michael Parenti, cited in Scott, *American War Machine,* 210.
51 For the following, see Wilson, "The Concept of the Parapolitical," passim.

reor, becomes a far-reaching and anticipatory security. *Ratio* becomes counting, calculating, calculus. *Ratio* is self-adjustment to what is correct."[52] In Heidegger's view — which, significantly, largely ignores the "suppressed" history of a more pluralistic attitude towards sovereignty within the Western tradition[53] — political "truth" that equates with rationality is both delimited by a unified discursive space and subjugated to the political will to domination: "The essence of truth as *veritas* [i.e., correctness] is *without space* and without ground,"[54] signifying the un-reality of the heterologous, or the "different"; "The result is the *presence* of truth as self-evidence, or the presence of thought to itself in the manner of self-identity" within an exclusively homogenous discursive space.[55] *Veritas* is the ground of Western jurisprudence's conflation of law with reason, establishing an undifferentiated chain of signifiers delimiting the parameters of "orthodox" or "common" legal speech. Correctness guarantees that whatever is not identical with *ratio* cannot constitute a portion of reality and, by political implication, cannot constitute an actual attribute of the "true" State. Consequently, "the idea of sovereignty, which clearly implies but one absolute power laying in the social order, with all relationships, all individuals […] ultimately subject to it, has been the characteristic approach to the political community."[56] Nationalism is secular mythology[57]: the onto-political division that originated with Plato serves as the historical originary of the modern nationalistic myth of the homogenous

---

52 Heidegger, *Parmenides*, 50.
53 "It has been the fate of pluralism in Western thought to take a rather poor second place to philosophies which make their point of departure the premise of, not the diversity and plurality of things, but, rather, some underlying unity and symmetry, needing only to be uncovered by pure reason to be then deemed the 'real,' the 'true,' and the 'lasting.'" Nisbet, *The Social Philosophers*, 386. Nisbet's language repeats the tenor of Platonic myth.
54 Ibid.
55 Bell, *Philosophy at the Edge of Chaos*, 28. "There is no space, no distance, between our true thoughts concerning a state of affairs in the world and that state of affairs: the two coincide." Ibid.
56 Nisbet, *The Social Philosophers*, 386.
57 See Anderson, *Imagined Communities*.

nation-state. With Hegel, "the transformation of *veritas* into *certitudo* is completed. This completion of the Roman essence of truth is the proper and hidden historical meaning of the nineteenth century."[58]

Although Heidegger situates the historical victory of political monism in the post-Napoleonic period, it is clear that ontopolitical monism — or what I have referred to as the indivisibility of sovereignty[59] — had achieved an irreversible ascendancy as early as the time of Jean Bodin (1529/30–1596), as has been established by Jens Bartelson.

> Since Bodin, indivisibility has been integral to the concept of sovereignty itself. In international political theory, this means that whenever sovereignty is used in a theoretical context to confer unity upon the state as an acting subject, all that it conveys is that this entity is an individual by virtue of its indivisibility [i.e., its monistic space], which is tautological indeed. What follows from this search for the locus of sovereignty in international political theory, however necessary to its empirical testability is thus nothing more than a logical sideshow; the essential step towards unity is already taken whenever sovereignty figures in the definition of political order. Whether thought to be upheld by an individual or a collective, or embedded in the State as a whole, sovereignty entails self-presence and self-sufficiency; that which is sovereign is immediately given to itself, conscious of itself, and thus acting for itself. That is, as it figures in international political theory, sovereignty is not an attribute of something whose existence is prior to or independent of sovereignty; rather, it is the concept of sovereignty itself which supplies this indivisibility and unity.[60]

---

58 Heidegger, *Parmenides*, 58.
59 Wilson, *The Savage Republic*.
60 Bartelson, *A Genealogy of Sovereignty,* 28. See also Wilson, *The Savage Republic*, 189–93.

But if we were to stand Bodin and the advocates of political monism "on their heads," we would notice immediately that the historically suppressed discourse of political pluralism identified by Nisbet[61] valorizes a political ontology of an equally potent and irreducible field of unassimilable heterogeneity. Hegel notwithstanding, it was the early modern nation-state that acted as the discursive space of the identity of unity with political power (*potestas*). The presence of unity/monism equates with the absence of pluralism, which is the multiplication, or proliferation, of political identities and entities. At the same time, however, the Platonic denial-of-difference contains within itself the very grounds of its actual reversal. The apparent falsity of the originary myth, the inversion of Bartelson's "empirical testability," is affirmed by the historical continuation of difference(s). As contemporary anti-Hegelian thought insists, the nation-state "is not best and fully understood as a teleological unity, directed exclusively at attending some single end or as having a single function"[62] — a profoundly parapolitical insight. In other words, the persistence of difference is itself the space of contestation with the Platonic myth; this is the central assumption of Heidegger's anti-Hegelian project. For Heidegger, "serious" — that is, metaphysical — thought within the post-Hegelian State demands a return to the early Hellenic concept of *alētheia* (the "un-concealed"[63]) that pre-dated *veritas*,[64] which is both the awareness and the actively making aware of the governing presence of ontology (Being) in all forms of thought and speech, "the uncommon within the common"; "For us, the matter of thinking is the Same, and this is Being — but Being with respect to its difference from beings."[65] Until this moment, what has been

---

61 See above, fn. 56.
62 Geuss, *History and Illusion in Politics*, 61.
63 That is, a non-correspondence notion of "truth."
64 Bell's commentary on this is excellent. "Truth as *aletheia*, as the unstable Being and clearing which allows for the presencing of thinking and being, is stabilised and replaced by the Roman view of truth as *veritas*, as correctness." Bell, *Philosophy at the Edge of Chaos*, 26.
65 Heidegger, *Identity and Difference*, 47; see also 50.

lacking in Western *logos* is the primacy of the heterogeneous, the "essential space of *aletheia,* the unconcealedness of things [...], a space completely covered over by debris and forgotten."[66] Ironically, the fatal flaw of the Heideggerian project lies within this very move towards the un-concealing of heterogeneity: whenever Heidegger attempts to convey a positive definition of Being, as opposed to the mere invocation of it, he reduces it to a self-identical and (re-)unifying "ideal of simplicity, purity and self-containment."[67] Being "is the unifying One, in the sense of what is everywhere primal and thus most universal; and at the same time it is the unifying One in the sense of the All-Highest (Zeus)."[68] "Truth" — that which is un-concealed — is difference, the being(s) within Being. However, within the Heideggerian schema, beings are ultimately revealed as embedded within the primordial and universal One. To think about Being as such is to repeat, on another level, the original sin of Platonism: the fetishizing of the (self-)identical. The true substitution of monism with heterogeneity demands a radical and unconditional rapprochement with difference(s)/being(s): *the proof of the absence of the homogenous is the signification of the presence of a potentially radical and discursively de-stabilizing heterogeneity that is irreducible to the human(-istic) domain of correctness.*

And such de-stabilization puts us squarely within the domain of both cosmic horror and, as I will show, its more respectable aesthetic twin: the *sublime.*

66 Heidegger, *Parmenides,* 50.
67 Bell, *Philosophy at the Edge of Chaos,* 150.
68 Heidegger, *Identity and Difference,* 69.

3. From the Sublime:
"The Call of Cthulhu" (1926)

> A subterrene voice or intelligence shouting monotonously in
> enigmatic sense-impacts undescribable save as gibberish.
> — H.P. Lovecraft

> We know how very difficult it is to interpret
> what is not understood.
> — Joaquim Fernandes and Fina D'Armada

The architect of the onto-epistemological foundations of what is (laughingly) known as "The Enlightenment," Immanuel Kant, "doubles" as modernity's premier aesthetician. This should come as no surprise, as Kant's entire metaphysical system ultimately serves an end both aesthetic and epistemological: to organize the world in such a way as to make it the grounds for objective understanding and absolute knowledge; in other words, to thoroughly serve "the purposive" — in Heideggerian terms, the reduction of both self and object to "correctness."[1]

For Kant, the perception of the world ("the transcendental deduction") requires a synthesis of what appears before us within both time and space. The synthetic project of "pure rea-

---

1 For an excellent short critique of Kant's anthropocentrism, see Budd, *The Aesthetic Appreciation of Nature*, 24–89. The entirety of Kant's aesthetics is predicated upon ontologically privileging *Homo sapiens* as a rational and autonomous moral agent.

son" requires three operational concepts, or "unities of synthesis": apprehension, reproduction, and recognition. Within the Kantian scheme, all knowledge and understanding is ultimately anthropocentric, in that all things must be reduced to "units of measure" that are compatible with human understanding (*cogito*); "A tree [the height of] which we estimate with reference to the height of a man, at all events gives us a standard for a mountain."[2] The categories of pure reason guaranteeing both the unity of phenomena as well as the ontological unity of the perceiving subject constitutes the "transcendental unity of apperception"[3]; "In other words, it is not so much that I perceive objects; it is rather my perception that presupposes the [unitary] object-form as one of its conditions."[4] For Kant, "the real (synthetic) formula of the cogito is: I think myself, and in thinking myself, I think that the object in general to which I relate a represented diversity."[5] Therefore, the operations of the *a priori* categories of synthetic understanding need to be supplemented by the work of an additional faculty, judgment, which is responsible for subordinating all of the inherent "sensible diversity" of spatio-temporal objects to the operational requirements of the synthetic categories of transcendental reason: "The only use which the understanding can make of these [concepts] is to judge by means of them."[6] From this follow two consequences, one phenomenological, the other aesthetic. In terms of the former, the human body itself is the final source not only of the units of measurement but of the operational constraints of the synthetic categories of pure reason.

> This primary (subjective, sensory, immediate, living) measure proceeds from the [human] body. And it takes the body as its primary object. […] *It is the body which erects itself as a measure.* It provides the measuring and measured unit of

2 Kant, *The Critique of Judgment*, 118.
3 Smith, "Translator's Introduction," xvii.
4 Ibid., xvi.
5 Deleuze, *Kant's Critical Philosophy*, cited in ibid., xvi.
6 Kant, cited in ibid., xvi.

measure: of the smallest and largest possible, of the minimum and the maximum, and likewise of the passage from the one to the other.[7]

In terms of the latter, the "lived evaluation" of space-time imparts a necessarily aesthetic dimension to judgment, as the operation of perception is inseparable from the appreciation and evaluation of form, which is the domain of the "aesthetic" properly defined; "All estimation of the magnitude of objects of nature is in the last resort aesthetic (i.e., subjectively and not objectively determined)."[8] And it is the intrinsically aesthetic nature of judgment that gives rise to one of Kant's seminal concepts: the *sublime*.[9] Although an aesthetic concept, the sublime is not identical with the beautiful; it is, in fact, largely antithetical to it. Whereas the beautiful dwells within the realm of intuition and the immediacy of perception — that is, the natural accordance of the spatio-temporal object with the synthetic categories of *cogito*[10] — the sublime is better understood as a form of sensory trauma, the catastrophic, or chaotic, sundering of the immediacy of perception from the transcendental unity of apperception.

> The Sublime, on the other hand, is to be found in a formless object, so far as in it or by occasion of it *boundlessness* is represented, and yet its totality is also present to thought. […]

---

7   Derrida, *The Truth in Painting*, 140.
8   Kant, cited in Smith, "Translator's Introduction," xviii.
9   Technically, Kant identifies two forms of the sublime: the mathematical, which is concerned with the spatial immensity of the natural world, and the dynamic, which is taken up with the immanency of physical forces. However, as Lovecraft implicitly treats the two forms interchangeably, giving equal emphasis to both the physical scale and the destructive powers of the Old Ones — the inhumanly large *monstrum* is always genocidally destructive — I shall follow suit and treat the Kantian sublime as a unity. See Lyotard, *Lessons on the Analytic*, 98–146.
10 "Natural beauty […] brings with it a purposiveness in its form by which the object seems to be, as it were, pre-adapted to our Judgment, and thus constitutes in itself an object of satisfaction." Kant, *The Critique of Judgment*, 102–3.

> [T]hat which excites in us, without any reasoning about it, but in the apprehension of it, the feeling of the sublime, may appear as regards its form to violate purpose in respect of the Judgment, to be unsuited to our presentative faculty, and, as it were, to do violence to the Imagination; and yet it is judged to be only the more sublime.[11]

Two aspects of Kant's notion of the sublime and their relevance to Lovecraftian poetics require comment.[12] Firstly, as we would expect, the Kantian sublime is remarkably, almost viscerally, phenomenological in nature: "Nature is therefore sublime in those of its phenomena whose intuition brings with it the Idea of its infinity."[13] Essential to the concept of the sublime is not merely the heightening of the *cogito*'s self-awareness of the grounding of perception upon the body, but the abject "insult" inflicted upon the anthropocentric unit of measurement: "We call that *sublime* which is *absolutely great*. […] [W]*hat is great beyond all comparison*. […] [T]*he sublime is that in comparison with which everything else is small.*"[14] Secondly, the subjective experience of the sublime is not the objective perception of the immediately unassimilable sensible diversity of the sublime object, but rather the traumatic inducement of a crisis of confidence in the witness's existential faith in the efficacy of judgment.

---

11   Ibid., 102–3. As the perceptive reader should be aware, this amounts to little more than a secularized version of *mysterium tremendum*; as Marjorie Hope Nicolson put it, "Awe, compounded of mingled terror and exultation, once reserved for God, passed over in the seventeenth century first to an expanded cosmos, then from the macrocosm to the greatest objects in the geo-cosmos — mountains, ocean, desert." Cited in Budd, *The Aesthetic Appreciation of Nature*, 66.

12   For two contrasting accounts of Lovecraft's treatment of the Kantian sublime, see Will, "H.P. Lovecraft and the Kantian Sublime" and Ralickas, "Cosmic Horror."

13   Kant, *The Critique of Judgment*, 116.

14   Ibid., 106 and 109. See Lyotard's commentary on this passage: "The infinite maximization of magnitudes leads to the Idea of an infinite magnitude, always already larger than any measurable magnitude. This magnitude is not numerable by recurrent addition of a unit to itself, however large it may be. It is off-limits to understanding." Lyotard, *Lessons on the Analytic*, 113.

[T]rue sublimity must be sought only in the mind of the [subject] judging, not in the natural Object, the judgment upon which occasions this state [...]. Consequentially it is the state of mind produced by a certain representation with which the reflective Judgment is occupied, and not the Object, that is to be called sublime.[15] [...] [T]*he sublime is that, the mere ability to think, which shows a faculty of the mind surpassing every standard of Sense.*[16]

One of the central artistic paradoxes of supernatural literature is the manner in which the weird tale combines (not always successfully) both subversive and reactionary elements; subversive because *ratio* is invariably threatened by the dramatically necessary presence of the Wholly Other/Monster, reactionary because the subversive presence is (nearly) always successfully challenged and eliminated. "Traditionally, genre horror is concerned with the irruption of dreadful forces into a comforting status quo — one which the protagonists frantically scrabble to preserve."[17] Lovecraft is one of the singular examples of the deployment of a counter-trend, largely through subliminal interrogation of *alētheia*: "By contrast, Lovecraft's horror is not one

---

15 On this point, see the commentary by Lyotard: "It follows from the fact that sublime judgment is reflective, as is the judgment upon the beautiful, that what is at stake is not the knowledge of the object, but the subjective sensation accompanying the presentation of the object." Ibid., 99.

16 Kant, *The Critique of Judgment*, 117 and 110. Emphasis in the original. Not surprisingly, Otto established a clear correlation, or a schematic association in "temporal sequence," between the Kantian sublime and the dualistic nature of the Holy. "Certainly we can tabulate some general 'rational' signs that uniformly recur as soon as we call an object sublime; as, for instance, the bounds of our understanding by some 'dynamic' or 'mathematic' greatness, by potent manifestations of force or magnitude in spatial extent. But these are obviously only conditions of, not the essence of, the impression of sublimity. A thing does not become sublime merely by being great. The concept itself remains unexplicated; it has in it something mysterious, and in this it is like that of the numinous." Otto, *The Idea of the Holy,* 41; see ibid., 41–49. In the end, Otto refuses to reduce religious experience to aesthetic sensation; ibid., 45–49.

17 Mieville, "Introduction," xiii.

of intrusion but of realization. The world has always been implacably bleak; the horror lies in our acknowledging that fact."[18] In Lovecraft's own words, "[T]he ultimate reality of space is clearly a complex churning of energy of which the human mind can never form any approximate picture, and which can touch us only through the veil of local apparent manifestations which we call the visible the material universe."[19]

As should now be obvious, these reflections clearly situate the Lovecraftian narrative within the domain of the Kantian aesthetic. Generically, all of Lovecraft's tales are variations of the comparatively early work "The Music of Erich Zann" (1921), a text that foregrounds the sublime in a remarkably surreptitious manner.

> [Zann] was trying to make a noise; to ward something off or drown something out — what, I could not imagine, awesome though I felt it must be... A sudden gust, stronger than the others, caught up the manuscript and bore it toward the window. I followed the flying sheets in desperation, but they were gone before I reached the demolished panes. Then I remembered my old wish to gaze from this window, the only window in the Rue d'Auseil[20] from which one might see the slope beyond the wall, and the city outspread beneath. It was very dark, but the city's lights always burned, and I expected to see them there amidst the rain and wind. Yet when I looked from that highest of all gable windows, looked while the candles sputtered and the insane viol howled with the night-wind, I saw no city spread below, and no friendly lights gleaming from the remembered streets, but only the blackness of space illimitable; unimagined space alive with motion and music, and having no semblance to anything on earth. And as I stood there looking in terror, the wind blew out

---

18 Ibid.
19 Cited in Martin, *H.P. Lovecraft*, 151.
20 Or *au seuil*, "at the threshold," denoting both liminality and nomadicism. Joshi, "Explanatory Notes," *Lovecraft, The Thing on the Doorstep*, 377.

both the candles in that ancient peaked garret, leaving me in savage and impenetrable darkness with chaos and pandemonium before me, and the daemon madness of that night-baying viol behind me. [21]

Significantly, the transition from the juvenile to the mature Lovecraft, the originating author of what became known as the Cthulhu Mythos, is signified by the transition from the orgiastic to the sublime and the grotesque. I discuss the defining elements of this term in more detail below. By general agreement, the canonical texts of the Mythos include — but may not be strictly limited to — "The Call of Cthulhu" (1926), "The Color Out of Space" (1927), "The Case of Charles Dexter Ward" (1927), "The Dunwich Horror" (1928), "The Whisperer in Darkness" (1930), "At the Mountains of Madness" (1931), "The Shadow over Innsmouth" (1931), "The Dreams in the Witch House" (1932), "The Shadow Out of Time" (1935), and "The Haunter of the Dark" (1936). In what follows, I will have to violate standard academic practice and provide what might be considered an excessive degree of reproduction of the original Lovecraftian texts. I consider this unavoidable: "His writing is so florid that it deserves to be quoted."[22] In the words of one of Lovecraft's most perceptive critics, Michel Houellebecq, "One might even say that the only reason for the often subtle and elaborate structure of Lovecraft's 'great texts' is to lay the groundwork for the stylistic explosion of these passages."[23] It is simply not possible to re-present the oblique in any terms other than itself.[24]

21 Lovecraft, "The Music of Erich Zann," 50–51. See Joshi's comment: " HPL considered the tale among his best, although in later years he noted that it had a sort of negative value: it lacked the flaws — notably over-explicitness and over-writing — that marred some of his other works, both before and after. It might, however, be said that HPL erred on the side of *under*-explicitness in the very nebulous horror seen through Zann's garret window." Ibid., 376.
22 Airaksinen, *The Philosophy of H.P. Lovecraft*, 40.
23 Houellebecq, *H.P. Lovecraft*, 88.
24 A point is not lost on Harman: "Lovecraft's major gift as a writer is his deliberate and skillful obstruction of all attempts to paraphrase him. No other

The decisive literary landmark is "The Call of Cthulhu," published in 1926, in which Lovecraft quite self-consciously presents himself as a conspiracy theorist — or, more precisely, a writer of conspiracy narratives: "The most merciful thing in the world, I think, is the inability of the human mind to correlate all of its contents."[25] With this justly famous opening line, the text clearly establishes itself as a detective story,[26] albeit one of a unique kind: the primary feat of ratiocination will not be the solving of a crime but the "penetrating" self-reflective interrogation of the Kantian aesthetic.

> We live on a placid island of ignorance in the midst of black seas of infinity, and it was not meant that we should voyage so far. The sciences, each straining in its own direction, have hitherto harmed us little; but some day the piecing together of disassociated knowledge will open up such terrifying vistas of reality, and of our frightful position therein, that we shall either go mad from the revelation or flee from the deadly light into the peace and safety of a new dark age.[27]

It is important to recall that, historically, the emergence of the detective story in the mid-19th century is inseparable from the development of conspiracy theory. The "conspiracy theorist in fact develops out of the classic detective"[28]; conversely, "a conspiracy theory narrative depends on the presence of a conspiracy theorist."[29] And the conspiracy theorist — the one who perceives (no matter how dimly) and announces (no matter how unpersuasively) the existence of a conspiracy — is, existentially,

---

    writer gives us monsters and cities so difficult to describe that he can only hint at their anomalies. […] [E]ven his own original words are already just the paraphrase of a reality that eludes all literal speech." Harman, *Weird Realism*, 9–10 and 54.

25 Lovecraft, "The Call of Cthulhu," 123.
26 Berruti, "H.P. Lovecraft and the Anatomy of Nothingness," 364. I discuss the detective novel in greater detail in the Conclusion.
27 Lovecraft, "The Call of Cthulhu," 123.
28 Wisnicki, *Conspiracy, Revolution, and Terrorism*, 18.
29 Ibid., 17.

in the exact same aesthetic dilemma as the experiential subject of the Kantian sublime: in both cases, the nature of the experience is a radical disorientation, as Lovecraft's narrator clearly attests to. The inability to endure the expansion of consciousness beyond the "correct" human unit of measure is a form of mercy:

> That is, *avoidance of cognitive dissonance by the compartmentalization and lack of communication* between facts stored in the human brain. It is merciful because *complete awareness of reality would almost certainly result in mental disintegration and psychosis.* […] Faced with the unutterable horror of total realization, Man is overwhelmed by a traumatic level of cognitive dissonance, and to reduce it not only denies reality, but also alters his belief in science, in progress, and in the future.[30]

Lovecraft's turn to a highly self-conscious form of conspiracy narrative clearly reflected an irresistible impulse to repudiate the humanistic overtones of the Kantian sublime: "The time has come when the normal revolt against time, space, & matter must assume a form not overtly incompatible with what is known as reality — when it must be gratified by images forming *supplements,* rather than *contradictions* of the visible & measurable universe."[31] It should by now be clear why the *monstrum* — the *sui generis,* or that thing which is without a species or category — constitutes a source of such profound psychic trauma. Embedded within the encounter with the Monster is the unconscious realization that the price that must be paid in order to fit the Wholly Other into some sort of categorical schema — representing a potentially vast inflation of the total set of classifications to the point of infinity — is the infliction of annihilating violence upon the *entirety* of our cognitive map.[32] It is precisely

---

30 Yozan Dirk W. Mossig, cited in Berruti, "H.P. Lovecraft and the Anatomy of Nothingness," 373. Italics in the original.
31 Lovecraft, cited in Joshi, "Introduction," xv.
32 For Noel Carroll, the cognitive problem of the Monster is the basis of its horror-inducing properties, or its "impurity"; "an *object* or *being* is impure

here that the inhumanly large of the sublime meets up with the humanly small of the grotesque: The Thing that is too big to comprehend (literally, "to see") is phenomenologically identical with the Thing that is too difficult to classify, as each produces their own type of terror and pain — a Burkean form of trauma. The artistic "price" to be paid for this unprecedented heightening of the uncanny effect of cosmic horror, "a kind of secular awe,"[33] is, of course, a corresponding intensification of collapse of faith in the synthetic faculties — an "occupational hazard" of the parapolitical scholar, as Scott's reflections upon 9/11 make clear: the chaotic irruption of a clandestine reality through a catastrophic event that resulted in the

> creation of a partly illusory mental space, in which unpleasant facts, such as that all western empires have been established through major atrocities, are conveniently suppressed. (I suspect in fact that most readers will be tempted to reject and forget [parapolitical events] [...] as something which simply "doesn't compute" with their observations of America.) I say this as one who believes passionately in civilization, and fears that by excessive denial our own civilization may indeed be becoming threatened.[34]

This striking similarity in tone between the disoriented Scott and Lovecraft's post-Kantian protagonist is readily explained by viewing both as a specifically modernist form of hero/narrator; as Art Berman has shown, modern "[a]rtistic self-conception is sheltered inside the modernist mind as a mode of alienation [...]. For the modernist artist [...] alienation is the most prominent level of self-consciousness, a principle feature of a

---

   if it is categorically interstitial, categorically contradictory, incomplete or formless." Carroll, *The Philosophy of Horror,* 32. "Thus, monsters are not only physically threatening; they are cognitively threatening. They are threats to common knowledge." Ibid., 34.

33 Ibid., 219, fn. 27.
34 Scott, *Deep Politics and the CIA Global Drug Connection,* 2–3. I will discuss the parapolitical trauma of 9/11 in more detail in Chapter Five.

personality surcharged with talent (or the supposition of talent) but politically powerless."[35] "The Call of Cthulhu," no less than Scott's parapolitical investigations, is pre-eminently a modernist text[36]; the defining element of literary modernism is an overriding concern (if not pre-occupation) with alienation, subjectivity, and absurdity, with the unifying element the disorientating disequilibrium that flows from a traumatizing cognitive dissonance induced by a "paradigm shift"[37] of some sort.

> In modernism, the consistent, linear narratives of traditional literature gave rise to forms that reflected the chaos of a fractured culture. Fragmented realities, failed communications, limited perspectives, and complicated histories are common in modernist texts, representing alienating subjectivity as a crucial subject of literary inquiry. [...] The concept of "denial of an absolute reality" indicates absurdity because logic depends upon a stable sense of reality. When reality is destabilized, logic is destabilized, and absurdity prevails.[38]

Hence

> [Modernism] is the one art that responds to the scenario of our chaos [...] of existential exposure to meaninglessness or absurdity. [...] [I]t is the art consequent on the dis-establishing of communal reality and conventional notions of causality, on the destruction of traditional notions of the wholeness of individual character, on the linguistic chaos that ensues

---

35 Berman, *Preface to Modernism*, 50.
36 Martin, *H.P. Lovecraft*, 84–90.
37 "Alternating paradigm shifts can be powerful vehicles for conveying concepts of subjectivity, disrupting the world views of traditional thinkers. One of the reasons that forced paradigm shifts are so disruptive is that the movement from one perspective to another is commonly seen as an admission of error in judgment rather than a sign of progress. It is due to this implication of fallibility that institutions tend to resist the dissemination of new information that contradicts the institution's previous claims and edicts." Ibid., 138–39.
38 Ibid., 39–40.

when public notions of language have been discredited and when all realities have become subjective fictions.[39]

By virtue of their modernist pedigree, the Lovecraftian protagonist is invariably a member of the "neurotic virtuosi,"[40] entrapped by their own alienation. [41] Alienation as "the shift from community to isolation, the transformation of the normal world to the abnormal world and accepted reality to an unacceptable reality"[42] qualifies the Lovecraftian narrator as the literary apotheosis of the conspiracy theorist: "Lovecraft's protagonists are virtually always placed in the position of facing their horrors alone, without consolation or even corroborating witnesses to the reality of their perceptions."[43] The methodological assumption of parapolitics is not that everything is "really" connected — the extreme, or deterministic, model of conspiracy theory — but that, certain things which would seem to be "separated" are, in fact, connected — appearances to the contrary. Therefore, as we should expect, the remarkably symmetrical tripartite narrative sequence of "The Call of Cthulhu"

---

39 Malcolm Bradbury and James McFarlane, cited in Martin, *H.P. Lovecraft*, 38.
40 Invariably a Schopenhauerian. "It is an unfortunate fact that the bulk of humanity is too limited in its mental vision to weigh with patience and intelligence those isolated phenomena, seen and felt only by a psychologically sensitive few, which lie outside common experience. Men of broader intellect know that there is no sharp distinction betwixt the real and the unreal; that all things appear as they do only by virtue of the delicate individual physical and mental media through which we are made conscious of them; but the prosaic materialism of the majority condemns as madness the flashes of super-sight which penetrate the common veil of obvious empiricism." Lovecraft, "The Tomb," 1.
41 Dziemianowicz, "Outsiders and Aliens," 169.
42 Martin, *H.P. Lovecraft*, 48.
43 Donald R. Burleson, cited in Dziemianowicz, "Outsiders and Aliens," 166. This is, of course, consistent with the signature but indispensable narrative technique of weird fiction, which is to "lay the foundation for the reader's suspension of disbelief by suggesting that the supernatural flourishes in the terra incognita of the rational world [...] [by] depriving the narrator of witnesses to corroborate his [*sic*] experience [...]. [The "weird" writer makes] the reader's belief an important part of the isolating technique." Ibid., 166.

embodies to perfection the credo (as well as the dilemma) of the investigator of parapolitical phenomena: "That glimpse, like all dread glimpses of truth, flashed out from an accidental piecing together of separated things [...]. I hope that no one else will accomplish this piecing out; certainly, if I live, I shall never knowingly supply a link in so hideous a chain."[44] As required by cosmic horror written within the post-Kantian age, the narrator must be mercilessly exposed to the a-holy terror of the sublime, but, to the exact same degree, be inhumanly (sadistically?) denied the salvific effect promised by Kant.[45] Stefan Dziemianowicz's incisive comments on the text are worth quoting in full.

> Probably the most important aspect of "The Call of Cthulhu" is the means by which [the narrator Francis Wayland Thurston] pieces together the clues and extrapolates what they imply. He is never an active participant in any of the story's three episodes. Although he travels to the places mentioned in the three accounts and sometimes interviews survivors, his discoveries mostly confirm what has already been recorded. His is basically a job of armchair deduction, from newspaper clippings that were no doubt read by others but that no one recognized as fitting a pattern. All these stories are described in such realistic, mundane detail [...] that anyone could have verified them had he seen the need to do so. This is Lovecraft's inversion of the transcendentalist notion that "there are sermons in stones." He says, in effect, that one does not need to investigate the dark corners of the universe to uncover mind-shattering cosmic truths; they may be evident in the events of the day if one knows the perspective from which to view the right events. The narrator's despair comes about simply through the *realization* of the pattern these events fit. In a sense, Lovecraft is expressing his belief

---

44 Lovecraft, "The Call of Cthulhu," 124.
45 See below.

that each one of us teeters on the brink of alienation along with Thurston.[46]

Consistent with the trope of modernism, in equal parts conspiratorial and anti-Kantian, the first tale of the Cthulhu Mythos cycle "revolves entirely around collaged documentation, being a framed collection of documents put together by the narrator."[47] In the first part of the tale, "The Horror in Clay,"[48] the narrator,[49] the nephew of George Gammell Angell, a recently deceased professor emeritus of Semitic languages at Brown University, discovers among his uncle's possessions a secret file of newsclippings of occultist incidents from around the world that all seem to corroborate the re-emergence of a trans-national underground religious cult centered upon the immanent return/resurrection of an obscene and genocidal atavistic "anti-God," CTHULHU.

> The press cuttings, as I have intimated, touched on cases of panic, mania, and eccentricity during the given period [Spring, 1925]. Professor Angell must have employed a cutting bureau, for the number of extracts was tremendous, and the sources scattered throughout the globe. Here was a nocturnal suicide in London, where a lone sleeper had leaped from a window after a shocking cry. Here likewise a rambling letter to the editor of a paper in South America, where a fanatic deduces a dire future from visions he has seen. A dispatch from California describes a theosophist colony as donning white robes en masse for some "glorious fulfillment" which never arrives, whilst items from India speak guardedly of se-

---

46 Dziemianowicz, "Outsiders and Aliens," 182.
47 Martin, *H.P. Lovecraft*, 84–85.
48 Lovecraft, "The Call of Cthulhu," 123–31.
49 In truth, the secondary and absent narrator. The heading immediately under the title of the text reads: "Found among the Papers of the Late Francis Wayland Thurston, of Boston." The real narrator of the tale, the "exonarrator" in Burleson's terms, is, in fact, the editor — presumably Lovecraft himself. Burleson, *Lovecraft*, 80.

rious native unrest toward the end of March. Voodoo orgies multiply in Hayti [*sic*], and African outposts report ominous mutterings. American officers in the Philippines find certain tribes bothersome about this time, and New York policemen are mobbed by hysterical Levantines on the night of March 22–23.[50] The west of Ireland, too, is full of wild rumor and legendry, and a fantastic painter named Ardois-Bonnot hangs a blasphemous "Dream Landscape" in the Paris salon of 1926. And so numerous are the recorded troubles in insane asylums that only a miracle can have stopped the medical fraternity from noting strange parallelisms and drawing mystified conclusions.[51] A weird bunch of cuttings, all told; and I can at this date scarcely envisage the callous rationalism with which I set them aside.[52]

The narrative device of enfolded unveiling — the uncovering of a hidden and/or repressed truth through the unravelling of multiple levels of written and/or oral evidence — is one of Lovecraft's most singular and important contributions to cosmic horror,[53] and, because of its obvious parallels with parapolitics and conspiracy,[54] needs to be examined in greater detail.

50 I take this as a reference to "The Horror of Red Hook," which was written the previous year and which, like "The Call of Cthulhu," demonstrates a pathological anxiety with racialized reverse colonization. See below.
51 A veiled reference to *Dracula*, a classic example of a horror text that doubles as a conspiracy narrative. See below.
52 Lovecraft, "The Call of Cthulhu," 131.
53 "The Call of Cthulhu" deploys "the technique of cut-and-paste in a pulp bricolage, aggregating a sense of dread and awe precisely out of the *lack* of over-arching plot. The exposition of a monstrous cosmic history, of hateful cults, of the misbehavior of matter and geometry, is all the stronger for being gradually, seemingly randomly, uncovered. […] Lovecraft's is not a fiction of carefully structured plot so much as of ineluctable unfolding: it is a literature of the inevitability of weird." Mieville, "Introduction," xii.
54 "In Lovecraft's prose collages, the collaged narratives and scraps of information are assembled by characters who only manage to find and fit together enough of the puzzle to become aware that the full picture is beyond their comprehension. In this sense, Lovecraft's alienating documents are not merely plot devices that introduce new information to the narrators. These

> Lovecraft's type of alienated scholar struggling to comprehend potentially world-changing documentation appears to be unique in "weird fiction." [...] [M]any of Lovecraft's narrators must struggle to understand new information through secondary sources alone, drawing attention toward the alienating influence of recorded information itself, removed from the first-hand shock of personal experience. The reader is challenged to scrutinize his or her own perceptions of reality, to face the fact that most ideas of reality are in fact based upon secondary sources.[55]

In his pioneering deconstructive analysis of Lovecraft, Donald Burleson strictly correlates the epistemological premise of the Lovecraftian tale with the "all wrong"; in aesthetic terms, of course, this means "irreducible to simple, stable terms."[56] On Burleson's own count, there are as many as nine layers of "epistemological strands" interweaving throughout the text,[57] each layer manifesting the intertwined representation of both one aspect of the conspiracy as well as the respective narrator's point of view, the "correctness" of which is fatally impaired by the overwhelming of the *cogito* by the unsolicited — and unexpected — visitation by the sublime. The total(-izing) effect of cognitive dissonance is multiplied not only by the plurality of the voices of the multitude of (traumatized and disoriented) witnesses but also by the manifestation of the self-same horrific sublime through the full array of artistic representation — literary, plastic, architectural, and musical. Not merely has synthetic unity been ruptured, but the un-mediated otherness of the sublime object (Cthulhu) has "invaded" or "appropriated" all forms of art. This represents an utterly daemonical critique of Kant — one that is, as far as I can tell, unrecognized within

---

documents form collages with their own implicit statements of subjectivity, revealing multiple limited perspectives on certain aspects of reality." Martin, *H.P. Lovecraft*, 139.

55 Ibid., 86.
56 Burleson, *Lovecraft*, 80.
57 Ibid.

"Lovecraft Studies." The aesthetic faculties, or imagination, are the *cogito*'s means of establishing the correctness of judgment and subjugating being to reason; if the a-holiness of Cthulhu's sublimity can be represented as the onto-epistemological foundation of a rival form of artistic expression, then not only is anthropocentric judgment merely finite, it is philosophically nonsensical. It is not merely the case that we are, in the very final instance, incapable of completely understanding the world; it is the case that truth itself is unconditionally anti-human.

Along with the cuttings are two other objects: a clay bas-relief of a weird hybrid animal–"god"[58] and a manuscript outlining the association between Professor Angell and the sculptor of the image, the "psychiatrically hyper-sensitive" artist Henry Anthony Wilcox.[59]

> Above these apparent hieroglyphs was a figure of evident pictorial intent, though its impressionistic execution forbade a very clear idea nature. It seemed to be a sort of monster, or symbol representing a monster, of a form which only a diseased fancy could conceive. If I say that my somewhat extravagant imagination yielded simultaneous pictures of an octopus, a dragon, and a human caricature, I shall not be unfaithful to the spirit of the thing. A pulpy, tentacled head surmounted a grotesque and scaly body of rudimentary wings;

---

58 In his important book *The Philosophy of Horror or Paradoxes of the Heart* (1990), Noel Carroll offers a binary classificatory scheme of the Monster: fusion and fission. "The central mark of a fusion figure is the compounding of ordinarily disjoint or conflicting categories in an integral, spatio-temporally unified individual," whereas fission divides *monstrum* into separate beings, either spatially or temporally, such as the Were-Wolf or the Shape-Shifter." Carroll, *The Philosophy of Horror*, 44 and 47. Great Cthulhu is Lovecraft's master-sign of fusion monstrosity; the animal–god's creator seems to have been addicted to fusion. Operating within the tradition of analytical philosophy, Carroll's generally impressive work is marred by the same problem as always: the privileging of epistemology at the expense of metaphysics. There is no doubt, as Lovecraft himself magnificently portends, that the Monster is an epistemic "problem"; this problem, however, is a symptom of an underlying difficulty in the nature of Being as such.

59 Lovecraft, "The Call of Cthulhu," 127.

> but it was the *general outline* of the whole which made it most shockingly frightful. Behind the figure was a vague suggestion of a Cyclopean architectural background.[60]

Wilcox conveniently offers his own interpretation of his bas-relief, adding an additional layer of self-reflexive communication as a "text-within-a-text"; "He said, 'It is new, indeed, for I made it last night in a dream of strange cities; and dreams are older than brooding Tyre, or the contemplative Sphinx, or garden-girdled Babylon.'"[61] This is immediately "cross-correlated" by Thurston, who usefully provides a pseudo-scientific corroboration of Wilcox's equally mystic/psychotic trance.

> It was then that he began that rambling tale which […] won the fevered interest of my uncle. There had been a slight earthquake tremor the night before [February 29, 1925], the most considerable felt in New England for some years; and Wilcox's imagination had been keenly affected. Upon retiring, he had an unprecedented dream of great Cyclopean cities of titan blocks and sky-flung monoliths, all dripping with green ooze and sinister with latent horror. Hieroglyphics had covered the walls and pillars, and from some undetermined point below had come a voice that was not a voice; a chaotic sensation which only fancy could transmute into sound, but which he attempted to render by the almost unpronounceable jumble of letters, "*Cthulhu fhtagn.*"[62]

Thurston then adds his self-reflexive commentary of his own estimation (*reor*) of Wilcox's displaced first-person confession.

> When Professor Angell became convinced that the sculptor was indeed ignorant of any cult or system of cryptic lore, he besieged his visitor with demands for future reports of

---

60 Ibid., 125–26.
61 Ibid., 127.
62 Ibid., 127–28.

dreams. This bore regular fruit, for after the first interview [March 1, 1925] the manuscript records daily calls of the young man, during which he related startling fragments of nocturnal imaginary whose burden was always some terrible Cyclopean vista of dark and dripping stone, with subterrene voice or intelligence shouting monotonously in enigmatical sense-impacts uninscribable save as gibberish. The two sounds frequently repeated are those rendered by the letters "*Cthulhu*" and "*R'lyeh*."[63]

Monumentalism is the architectonic expression of the will-to-totalitarianism. Not only is the Cyclopean one of the primary signifiers of the anti-human Cthulhu (fascism as the "suspension" of democracy) but, in Lovecraft's conspiratorial narrative strategies, monumental structures are fully capable of inducing that epistemic rupture that is the sign of the sublime. As Houellebecq astutely observes,

Hence all impressionism must be banished to build a vertiginous literature; and without a certain *disproportionality of scale,* without the juxtaposition of the minute and the limitless, the punctual and the infinite, there can be no vertigo. […] [Lovecraft] wants to create a sense of precarious balance; the characters move between precise coordinates, but they are oscillating at the edge of the abyss.[64]

63 Ibid.
64 Houellebecq, *H.P. Lovecraft,* 79. See also ibid. at 65 and 66: "For like the great Gothic or baroque cathedrals, the dream architecture he describes is a total architecture. […] H.P. Lovecraft's architecture, like that of the great cathedrals, like that of Hindu temples, is much more than a three-dimensional mathematical puzzle. It is entirely imbued with an essential dramaturgy that gives its meaning to the edifice. That dramatizes the very smallest spaces that uses the conjoint resources of the various plastic arts that annexes the magic play of light to its own ends. It is living architecture because at its foundation lies a living and emotional concept of the world. In other words, it is sacred architecture." As Houellebecq laconically remarks, "Howard Phillips Lovecraft was amongst those few men who experience a

As with architecture, so it is with both music and dance. The second part of Angell's manuscript, "The Tale of Inspector Legrasse,"⁶⁵ recounts an earlier — albeit equally secondhand — encounter with the Cthulhu cult. In 1908, Inspector John Raymond Legrasse of the New Orleans Police Department solicits information from the delegates of the American Archaeological Society holding its annual meeting in St. Louis. Legrasse brings with him a small statue of the cephalopod animal–god and recounts his recent investigation of a murderous Voodoo cult.

> On November 1st, 1907, there had come to the New Orleans parish a frantic summons from the swamp and lagoon country to the south. The squatters there [...] were in the grip of stark terror from an unknown thing which had stolen upon them in the night. It was voodoo, apparently, but voodoo of a more terrible sort than they had ever known; and some of their women and children had disappeared since the malevolent tom-tom had begun its incessant beating far within the black haunted woods where no dweller ventured. There were insane shouts and harrowing screams, soul-chilling chants and dancing devil-flames; and, the frightened messenger added, the people could stand it no more.⁶⁶

Not at all unlike the U.S. Army in Afghanistan, Legrasse and his men intervene.⁶⁷ Not surprisingly, and again not unlike the U.S. Army in Afghanistan, what Legrasse et al. encounter is the "nameless."

> Only poetry or madness [!] could do justice to the noises heard by Legrasse's men as they ploughed on through the

---

violent trance-like state where they look at beautiful architecture." Ibid., 65. This seems to be a constant personality trait of the fascist.

65   Lovecraft, "The Call of Cthulhu," 132–45.
66   Ibid., 136.
67   Ibid., 136–39.

black morass toward the red glare of the muffled tom-toms.[68] [...] In the natural glade of the swamp stood a grassy island of perhaps an acre's extent, clear of trees and tolerably dry. On this now leaped and twisted a more indescribable horde of human abnormality. [...] Void of clothing, this hybrid spawn were braying, bellowing, and writhing about a monstrous ring-shaped bonfire; in the center of which, revealed by occasional rifts in the curtain of flame, stood a great granite monolith some eight feet in height; on the top of which, incongruous in its diminutiveness, rested the noxious carven statuette.[69] From a wide circle of scaffolds set up at regular intervals with the flame-girt monolith as a center hung, head downward, the oddly marred bodies of the helpless squatters who had disappeared. It was inside this circle that the ring of worshippers jumped and roared, the general direction of the mass motion being from left to right in endless Bacchanal between the ring of bodies and the ring of fire.[70]

Legrasse's round-up nets a motley collection of typically racialist grotesques — "examined at headquarters after a trip of intense strain and weariness, the prisoners all proved to be men of a very low, mixed-blooded, and mentally aberrant types"[71] — but, more importantly, the first allegedly "true" revelations of the nature of the Cthulhu cult: "They worshipped, so they said, the

68 Ibid., 137.
69 "The statuette is described as being between seven to eight inches in height and of exquisitely artistic workmanship. It represented a monster of vaguely anthropoid outline, but with an octopus-like head whose face was a mass of feelers, a scaly, rubbery-looking body, prodigious claws on hind and fore feet, and long, narrow wings behind. This thing, which seemed instinct with a fearsome and unnatural malignancy, was of a somewhat bloated corpulence, and squatted evilly on a rectangular block or pedestal covered with undecipherable characters [...]. They, like the subject matter, belonged to something horribly remote and distinct from mankind as we know it; something frightfully suggestive of old and unhallowed cycles of life in which our world and conceptions have no part." Ibid., 133–34.
70 Ibid., 138.
71 Ibid., 139.

Great Old Ones who lived ages before there were any men, and who came to the young world out of the sky."[72] A hybridity, then, of the supernatural and the extra-terrestrial; one is reminded of Arthur C. Clarke's famous observation that a sufficiently advanced technology would be indistinguishable from magic. In truth, the Mythos appears to be premised upon a daemonic inversion of Clarke's dictum: a sufficiently advanced form of magic would be indistinguishable from science.

> Those Old Ones were gone now, inside the earth and under the sea; but their dead bodies had told their secrets in dreams to the first men, who formed a cult which had never died. This was that cult, and the prisoners said it had always existed and always would exist, hidden in distant waters and dark places all over the world until the time when the great priest Cthulhu, from his dark house in the mighty city of R'lyeh under the waters, should rise and bring the earth again beneath his sway. Some day he would call, when the stars were ready, and the secret cult would always be waiting to liberate him.[73]

"Dead bodies" is an anthropocentric construction; in fact, the Great Old Ones are in a temporary state of stasis, or hibernation, the active/dormant life-phases of the extraterrestrials governed by aeon-spanning astronomical cycles: in other words, temporal units of an inhuman order of magnitude.

> These Great Old Ones [...] were not composed altogether of flesh and blood. They had shape [...] but that shape was not made of matter. When the stars were right, They could plunge from world to world through the sky; but when the stars were wrong, They could not live. But although They no longer lived, They would never really die. They all lay in stone houses in Their great city of R'lyeh, preserved by the spells of mighty Cthulhu for a glorious resurrection when

---

72 Ibid.
73 Ibid.

the stars and the earth might once more be ready for Them. But at that time some force from outside must serve to liberate Their bodies. The spells that preserved them intact likewise prevented them from making an initial move, and They could only lie awake in the dark and think whilst uncounted millions of years rolled by. They knew all that was occurring in the universe, for Their mode of speech was transmitted thought. Even now They talked in their tombs. When, after infinities of chaos, the Great Old Ones spoke to the sensitive among them by moulding their dreams; for only thus could Their language reach the fleshy minds of mammals.[74]

The Great Old Ones suffer a double exile not only in time but in space; their bodies are entombed alongside that of their heresiarch Cthulhu, himself enveloped by the walls of his Cyclopean metropolis: "The great stone city of R'lyeh, with its monoliths and sepulchers, had sunk beneath the waves; and deep waters, full of the one primal mystery through which not even thought can pass, had cut off the spectral intercourse."[75]

Finally revealed for us is the central conceit of the overarching storyline of Lovecraft's late period: the Cthulhu Mythos, itself a pun on "chthonic,"[76] is premised upon the extra-dimensional covert machinations of a clandestine anti-pantheon, the Cthonoi, whose members include (but are not limited to) SHUB-NIGGURATH THE BLACK GOAT OF THE WOODS WITH A THOUSAND YOUNG; HASTUR THE DESTROYER; YUGGOTH; TSATHO-GGUA; NYARLATHOTEP; AZATHOTH; and YOG-SOTHOTH. As Lovecraft makes clear in one of his last stories:

> Even now I refused to believe what he [the Whisperer in Darkness] implied about the constitution of ultimate infin-

[74] Ibid., 140–41.
[75] Ibid., 141.
[76] "The irrational in Lovecraft's tales seems indissociable from the images of the depths. The abnormal, the disquieting, and the unclean are, on the vertical axis of the imagination, always situated toward the bottom, in the zone of the deepest shade." Levy, *Lovecraft*, 64.

ity, the juxtaposition of dimensions, and the frightful of our known cosmos of space and time in the unending chain of linked cosmos-atoms which makes up the immediate super-cosmos of curves, angles, and material and semi-material electronic organization [...]. I started with loathing when told of the monstrous nuclear chaos beyond angled space which the *Necronomicon* has mercifully cloaked under the name of Azathoth. It was shocking to have the foulest nightmares of secret myth cleared up in concrete terms whose stark, morbid hatefulness exceeded the boldest hints of ancient and mediaeval mystics.[77]

At the end of his career, Lovecraft finally revealed the Great Old Ones as the personifications of what we would denote as "quantum weirdness." In Houellebecq's insightful commentary:

These are the coordinates of the unnamable. This is not a coherent mythology, precisely drawn; it is unlike Greco-Roman mythology or this or that magical pantheon whose very clarity and *finitude* is almost reassuring. These Lovecraftian entities remain somewhat tenebrous. He avoids precision with regards to the distribution of their powers and abilities. In fact, their exact nature is beyond the grasp of the human mind. The impious books that pay homage to them and celebrate their cult do so in confused and contradictory terms. They remain fundamentally *unutterable*. We only get fleeting glimpses of their hideous power; and those humans who seek to know more ineluctably pay in madness or in death.[78]

But equally so are the Great Old Ones the mytho-poetic personifications of the clandestine attributes and agencies of the stereotypical conspiracy narrative. As Legrasse's degenerate informants tell him,

---

77 Lovecraft, "The Whisperer in Darkness," 218–19.
78 Houellebecq, *H.P. Lovecraft*, 83.

That cult would never die till the stars came right again, and the secret priests would take great Cthulhu from His tomb to revive His subjects and resume His rule of earth. The time would be easy to know, for then mankind would have become as the Great Old Ones; free and wild and beyond good and evil, with laws and morals thrown aside and all men shouting and killing and reveling in joy. Then the liberated Old Ones would teach them new ways to shout and kill and revel and enjoy themselves, and all the earth would flame with a holocaust of ecstasy and freedom. Meanwhile the cult, by appropriate rites, must keep alive the memory of those ancient ways and shadow forth the prophecy of their return.[79]

Houellebecq's comment on this passage is priceless: "This is just a frightening paraphrase of Saint Paul."[80] But it is a heretical inversion of Pauline eschatology that takes us uncannily close to the conspiratorial: Cthulhu's conspiracy against humankind — the instigation of a global race war waged by the grotesque "lower orders" by means of long-range telepathic suggestion (mind-control-at-a-distance being the coded meaning of the "Call" of the title) is a quintessential theme of the Lovecraftian conspiracy narrative.[81] The centrality of the trope of conspiracy is reenforced by the marked similarity between Cthulhu's degenerate worshippers and the grotesque anarchists treated by G.K. Chesteron in one of the seminal texts of conspiracy literature, *The Man Who Was Thursday* (1908). The identity-shifting leader of the anarchists, Lucian Gregory, "seemed like a walking blasphemy, a blend of the angel and the ape."[82] And his propensity for the politics of the apocalypse puts him squarely within the camp of the bacchanal negroids of the Louisiana swamps.

---

79 Lovecraft, "The Call of Cthulhu," 141.
80 Houellebecq, *H.P. Lovecraft*, 113.
81 One that has proven of remarkable duration; among other things, it serves as the main plot device of the seminal Hammer Studios production *Five Million Years to Earth* (1967), a film that is strikingly Lovecraftian in its sensibilities.
82 Chesterton, *The Man Who Was Thursday*, 3.

> "My red hair, like red flames, shall burn up the world," said Gregory [...]. Then out of this unintelligible creature the last thunders broke [...]. "You are the Law, and you have never been broken. But is there a free soul alive that does not long to break you, only because you have never been broken? We in revolt talk all kind of nonsense doubtless about this crime or that crime of the Government. It is all folly! The only crime of the Government is that it governs. The unpardonable sin of the supreme power is that it is supreme."[83]

Lovecraft's affinity with conspiracy narrative, in fact, goes far beyond Chesterton; when read closely, it is clear that "The Call of Cthulhu" falls under the literary classification of reverse colonization, placing the text within the same league of other conspiratorial classics such as Bram Stoker's *Dracula* and H.G. Well's *The Time Machine* and *The War of the Worlds*.[84] A popular sub-genre in late Victorian and Edwardian literature, the reverse colonization narrative was suffused with "the sense that the entire [Anglo-Saxon] nation — as a race of people, as a political and imperial force, as a social and cultural power — was in irretrievable decline."[85] The generic reverse colonization narrative manifests two overriding concerns: guilt (of the genocidal depredations of imperialism — "all western empires have been established through major atrocities," in Scott's words — with the counter-invasion a form of retributive justice) and fear (namely, the overthrow of the decadent master race by the stealth and the feral virility of the colonized peoples). Given his neurotic racism, it is not surprising that guilt is largely absent from Lovecraft's weird tales.[86] This omission is more than compensated for, however, by the abjectly hysterical (and histrionic) expression of fear; as with the very "best" of the reverse colonization fantasists, Lovecraft is "obsessed with the spectacle of the primitive and the

---

83 Ibid., 176.
84 Wisnicki, *Conspiracy, Revolution, and Terrorism*, 173–79.
85 Arata, "The Occidental Tourist," 622.
86 See below.

atavistic."[87] In Lovecraft, as with Stoker and Wells, a "terrifying reversal has occurred: the colonizer finds himself in the position of the colonized, the exploiter becomes exploited, the victimizer victimized. Such fears are linked to a perceived decline — racial, moral, spiritual — which makes the nation vulnerable to attack from more vigorous, 'primitive' peoples."[88] And, in truth, the more we examine "The Call of Cthulhu," the more traces of reverse colonization we can find. From the St. Louis meeting with Legrasse, Angell gains knowledge of two additional facts which are central to both Cthulhu's conspiracy and the overarching plotline of the later installments of the mythos. The first is that a "forbidden book" is the hermeneutic key to understanding the entirety of the cult: the *Necronomicon*,[89] authored by the "mad Arab Abdul Al-Hazred"[90] in whose brain-blasting words

That is not dead which can eternal lie,
And with strange aeons even death may die.[91]

The *Necronomicon* stipulates that the center of the Cthulhu cult "lay amid the pathless desert of Arabia, where Irem, the City of Pillars [Persepolis], dreams hidden and untouched. It was not allied to the European witch-cult, and was virtually unknown beyond its members."[92] This leads to the second vital point: that the Cthulhu cult is truly cosmopolitan, preposterously extending all the way to the Arctic. During the St. Louis meeting, William Channing Webb, Professor of Anthropology, Princeton University, relates to Legrasse and company that an earlier expedition in 1860 to West Greenland had uncovered

---

87 Arata, "The Occidental Tourist," 624.
88 Ibid., 623.
89 The master-sign of the Cthulhu Mythos in the form of a diabolic parody of *The Rubaíyát of Omar Khayyám*, the Lovecraftian tome was clearly inspired by Robert W. Chamber's equally melodramatic fictitious brain-blasting/ insanity-inducing theatrical script, *The King in Yellow.*
90 Grammatically incorrect; in Arabic, his name should be Abd-al-Hazred. Burleson, *Lovecraft*, 49. I discuss Al-Hazred in greater detail below.
91 Lovecraft, "The Call of Cthulhu," 142.
92 Ibid.

> [a] singular tribe or cult of degenerate Esquimaux whose religion, a curious form of devil-worship, chilled him with its deliberate bloodthirstiness and repulsiveness. It was a faith of which other Esquimaux knew little, and which they mentioned only with shudders, saying that it had come down from horribly ancient aeons before ever the world was made.[93]

Even more uncannily (or brain-blasting, if you prefer) is the only-just-now recognized fact that the main ritualistic chant of the diabolical Inuits is identical with that of the sub-human negroids of the New Orleans Voodoo cult. To wit:

> *Ph'nglui mglw' nafh Cthulhu R'leyh wgah' nagl fhtagn.*
> *In his house at R'lyeh dead Cthulhu waits dreaming.*[94]

According to Thurston, there then "followed an exhaustive comparison of details, and a moment of awed silence when both detective and scientist agreed on the virtual identity of the phrase common to two hellish rituals so many worlds of distance apart."[95]

It is important to note here an under-appreciated convergence between this text and the earlier weird tale "The Music of Erich Zann": both rely upon the notion of a "symphonic correspondence" to aesthetically convey the sense of an immeasurable sublime.

> It may have been only imagination and it may have been only echoes which induced one of the men, an excitable Spaniard, to fancy he heard antiphonal responses to the ritual from some far and unilluminated spot deeper within the wood of ancient legendary horror. This man, Joseph D. Galvez, I later met and questioned; and he proved distractingly imaginative.

---

93 Ibid., 134.
94 Ibid., 135.
95 Ibid.

> He indeed went so far as to hint of the faint beating of great wings, and of a glimpse of shining eyes and a mountainous white bulk beyond the remotest trees — but I suppose he had been hearing too much native superstition.[96]

Lovecraft both supplements and explicates the nebulous and "orgiastic" horrors of the earlier text through the deployment of a series of parapolitical metaphors and images in the latter: specifically, the "global conspiracy." In other words, by re-locating Zann's cosmic Other to the material plane but extending it through terrestrial time and space, Cthulhu's global race conspiracy is rendered tantamount to the sublime: an infinite multiplication of social connections (a "social multitude" that is a form of magnitude) throughout space-time (Providence, Greenland, New Orleans, Norway, New Zealand) yields an alien presence that ruptures synthetic unity — that is, an aesthetic conceit that is affectively identical to the sublime.

> It would be both useless and disturbing to repeat all that we concluded; but I may hint that we agreed in believing that we had secured a clue to the source of some of the most repulsive primordial customs in the cryptic elder religions of mankind. It seemed plain to us, also, that there were ancient and elaborate alliances between the hidden outer creatures and certain members of the human race. How extensive these alliances were, and how their state today might compare with their state in earlier ages, we had no means of guessing; yet at best there was room for a limitless amount of horrified speculation. There seemed to be an awful, immemorial linkage in several definite stages betwixt man and nameless infinity. The blasphemies which appeared on earth, it was hinted, came from the dark planet Yuggoth [Pluto], at the rim of the solar system; but this was itself merely the populous outpost of a frightful interstellar race whose ultimate source must lie

---

96 Ibid., 138.

far outside even the Einsteinian space-time continuum or greatest known cosmos.[97]

The conspiracy narrative, through its vital connection with the detective narrative, is thoroughly modernist in its construction. Most indicative of its modernist "prejudice," however, is the conspiracy tale's reliance upon Darwinism: "Darwin's theory was revolutionary [...] because although he took up the '*old* problems' of 'chance, environment, death, [and] survival,'" he moved away from the "'leaps' of the chain of being 'with its hierarchical ordering of rungs' and towards the ecological image of the 'inextricable web of affinities.' Darwin, in other words, de-centered man in favor of the complex network of nature."[98] Understood as an unending proliferation of "inextricable webs of affinities," the Darwinian imaginary formed part of the modernist vocabulary of the Victorian conspiracy novel that invested it with a determinative albeit subliminal imaginative sense of the sublime.

> In their most typical version, conspiracy theory narratives depict a conspiracy that defies genre categorization (e.g., only a foreign invader or revolutionary group) and spatial location (operating in Germany or in London, etc.) because the conspiracy is *everywhere,* because it has grown to the extent of being *generalized,* potentially *indeterminate,* and even *beyond the conscious control or knowledge of its conspirators.*[99]

The conspiratorial aesthetic is most clearly put on display in the third part of the tale, "The Madness From the Sea."[100] Here, Thurston recounts his reading of the journal of a recently deceased Norwegian ship captain, Gustaf Johansen, the only survivor of an encounter on March 23, 1925, with a mysterious, unchartered island in the far southern Pacific Ocean (S. Latitude 47°9´; W.

---

97 Lovecraft, "The Whisperer in Darkness," 185.
98 George Levine, cited in Wisnicki, *Conspiracy, Revolution, and Terrorism*, 60.
99 Wisnicki, *Conspiracy, Revolution, and Terrorism*, 9.
100 Lovecraft, "The Call of Cthulhu," 145–57.

Longitude 126°43´), which turns out to be the prematurely (and only temporarily) re-surfaced city of R'lyeh and a partially awoken Cthulhu, now revealed as the direct source of the concurrent "wave" of psychic distortions experienced by Atkins and the other "sensitives." Through Johansen we learn that the genocidal arch-priest of the Old Ones is able to leave stasis for a short time because of a localized earthquake that brings part of R'leyh to the surface; in Houellebecq's memorable summary of this cataclysmic event, "Between 4:00 pm and 4:15 pm a breach occurred in the architecture of time. And through the fissure created, a terrifying entity manifested itself on our earth."[101] The imagery here is highly evocative of the conspiratorial presence — exactly as with Walter Cronkite solemnly intoning the precise time and place of the death of John F. Kennedy, the journalistic reportage frames the exact moment of the irruption of the parapolitical into the social consensus of public perception.[102] And, of course, this unveiling of the parapolitical nameless is identical with epistemological crisis and cognitive disaster: "The very sun of heaven seemed distorted when viewed through the polarizing miasma welling out from this sea-soaked perversion, and twisted menace and suspense lurked leeringly in those crazily elusive angles of carven rock where a second glance shewed concavity after the first shewed convexity."[103] In a striking manner, Lovecraft signifies the catastrophic annihilation of "common sense" through the equally violent re-assertion of the antithetical architectonic: "As Wilcox would have said, the geometry of the place was all wrong. One could not be sure that the sea and the ground were horizontal, hence the relative position[104]

---

101 Houellebecq, *H.P. Lovecraft*, 82.
102 See Houellebecq on exactly this point. "If distant entities that are several hundred million years old appear in the course of our human history, it is vital to document the exact moments of their appearance. Each point is a rupture. To allow the unutterable to erupt." Ibid., 78–79.
103 Lovecraft, "The Call of Cthulhu," 153.
104 "Under the cover of the theory of relativity [...] Lovecraft's tales are, in a way, only a vast attempt at the dramatization of space, rendered agonizing by his dynamics, and fantastic insofar as its unforeseeable metamorphoses come to trouble the Euclidean order of things. [...] The known world, the

of everything else seemed phantasmally variable."[105] (It should be pointed out here that the frequent "name-dropping" of Einstein and the repeated sophomoric references to the Theory of Relativity is a crucial literary gimmick of Lovecraft; in addition to investing his "post-supernatural" weird tales with a veneer of largely erroneous pseudo-scientific respectability, Einsteinian physics served as a useful artifact of popular culture that invests radical post-Kantian metaphysics with a "hip" plausibility that enables the sophomoric "educated" reader to enter more easily into the dramatic landscape of the fiction.[106]) The noumenal reality of the Great Old Ones is re-presented as the sublime space by their "impossible" architecture, which doubles as Lovecraft's "rapture" of the a-holy numinous.[107]

Two things are of particular note in this remarkable passage, arguably the apex of Lovecraft's literary career, and both cast further light upon Lovecraft's sophisticated engagement with Kantian aesthetics. The first is that Lovecraft shows an astute grasp of Kant's vital distinction between the sublime properly-so-called and the merely monstrous. According to Kant, if "that magnitude of a natural Object [...] is great beyond all standards of sense, it makes us judge as *sublime*, not so much the object, as our own state of mind in the estimation of it."[108] In other words, the sublime, although clearly related to inhuman magnitude,

> universe of the charts and maps, is but a negligible part of 'total reality,' of that space-time continuum Einstein alone perceived." Levy, *Lovecraft*, 52.

105 Lovecraft, "The Call of Cthulhu," 153–54.
106 "The references to Einstein are there merely to justify crudely and superficially an action whose purpose is the hazardous, hesitant exploration of the utter depths of the psyche. The reader must feel disoriented, lost, and powerless, and what better way to reach this end than to make him enter the thousand and one labyrinths of a delirium [...] knowingly controlled? Only when the familiar setting collapses can the fantastic adventure begin." Levy, *Lovecraft*, 53.
107 "It is a well-known fact that disorder is at the very source of the fantastic. This suspension of natural laws can be manifested, as far as space is concerned, only by an alteration of perspective and proportion." Ibid., 45. The "nightmarish" architectural illustrations of Giovanni Piranesi (1720–88) who, not coincidentally, was a favorite of Lovecraft, are a case in point.
108 Kant, *The Critique of Judgment*, 117.

is not reducible to it: rather, the aesthetic truth, sublime, as a highly idiosyncratic instance of the judgment, lies with its transformative capacity of the *cogito*'s experience of perception.

> An object is *monstrous* if by its size it destroys the purpose which constitutes the concept of it. But the mere presentation of a concept is called *colossal,* which is almost too great for any presentation (bordering on the relatively monstrous); because the purpose of the presentation of a concept is made hard [to carry out] by the intuition of the object being almost too great for our faculty of apprehension.[109]

If the monstrous object is of such magnitude (or otherness) as to be objectively irreducible to the unifying effect of judgment, then it is not properly an object of aesthetic experience as such — it signifies the outermost extremity of human comprehension and, thereby, remains inherently unassimilable. But whereas for Kant this represents a crisis of perception, and the end of intelligible aesthetic experience, for Lovecraft this is the entire point: the over-turning of anthropocentrism, the Holy Grail of cosmic horror, through the dramatic violence of alien confrontation and incomprehension. Cthulhu is the master-sign of the "Thing [that] cannot be described — there is no language for such abysms of shrieking and immemorial lunacy, such eldritch contradictions of all matter, force, and cosmic order."[110] In that sense, Lovecraft is actually much closer to the narrative intuitions of Chesterton than to the more formal philosophical speculations of Kant; compare, for example, Lovecraft's trauma-

---

109 Ibid., 123. Compare this passage with Levy's comment on the literary significance of Lovecraftian monstrosity: "To enter Lovecraft's fantastic universe is to be brutally dislodged from the familiar, dispossessed of all criteria or systems of reference, violently thrown into an abnormal space amid beings of which the least one can say is that they transgress the common order. The monster plays no negligible role in this basic bewilderment; it surprises, it frightens, it shocks." Levy, *Lovecraft*, 55. Both Lovecraft and Kant problematize the issue of scale in a decisive manner.

110 Lovecraft, "The Call of Cthulhu," 154.

inducing portrayal of Cthulhu-as-the-nameless with the final description of Sunday offered by Chesterton's protagonist Gabriel Syme:

> As he gazed, the great face grew to an awful size, grew larger than the colossal mask of Memnon, which had made him scream as a child. It grew larger and larger, filling the whole sky; then everything went black. Only in the blackness before it entirely destroyed his brain he seemed to hear a distant voice saying a commonplace text that he had heard somewhere, "Can ye drink of the cup that I drink of?"[111]

Cthulhu is not sublime in itself; rather, it is the brain-blasting encounter with the Wholly Other/Monster that gives rise to the subjective experience of the colossal within the witnesses. And it is here that Lovecraft inflicts his most decisive parodic twist of Kant: he treats the psychic trauma inflicted by the sublime with the *alētheia* furnished by the weird tale — and by the conspiracy narrative.

The popular resistance to the conspiratorial notion of governmental complicity in the terrorist massacres of 9/11 that so disoriented Scott is grounded at least as much on aesthetic principles as political or moral — as with the sunken cyclopean city of R'lyeh, the (para-)political geometry of the Deep State "is not right"; the dots of cognition cannot be connected by straight lines precisely because the curvature of space and time are "all wrong."[112] The signature parapolitical poetics of Scott and his emphasis upon the irrationality of the Dual State are strikingly psychoanalytical in nature, creating (perhaps deliberately) a series of meaningful associations: repression, denial, the unconscious, guilt, transference. Missing though, but synonymous with all of the above, is the notion of *dream* — precisely that which is the

---

[111] Chesterton, *The Man Who Was Thursday*, 177.
[112] For two well-received accounts of 9/11 as both a conspiratorial act of the Bush administration and a collective exercise in the traumatic inducement of cognitive dissonance, see Griffith, *The New Pearl Harbor*, and Griffith and Scott, *9/11 and American Empire*.

sine non qua of the weird tale.¹¹³ Revealingly, "dream" in German is *Traum,* which evokes "trauma"; trauma, in turn, is etymologically derived from the Greek word for "wound," a rupturing-by-force that serves as sign of combat and violence. If the essence of neurosis is conflict, then every act of repression is a self-inflicted wound; every dream that symbolically announces the presence of the repressed is a signifier of trauma. In terms of Kant's aesthetic, 9/11, for example, may be considered a "sublime" event.

> The effort, therefore, to receive in one single intuition a measure for magnitude that requires a considerable time to apprehend, is a kind of representation, which, subjectively considered, is contrary to [anthropocentric] purpose: but objectively, as requisite for the estimation of magnitude, it is purposive. Thus that very violence which is done to the subject through the Imagination is judged as purposive *in reference to the whole* determination of the mind. The quality of the feeling of the Sublime is that it is a feeling of pain in reference to the faculty by which we judge aesthetically of an object. […] The feeling of the Sublime is therefore a feeling of pain, arising from the want of accordance between the aesthetical estimation of magnitude formed by the Imagination and the estimation of the same formed by Reason.¹¹⁴

In studied contrast, the signature scream of the Lovecraftian protagonist is the traumatic "bodily" realization of the irretrievable loss of the transcendental unity of apperception; the phenomenological expression of the irreparable rupture of the synthetic unities of the faculties of perception.

---

113 "To our mind, the fantastic is born from the divorce produced between the perfect lucidity of the characters and the dream-images that they encounter. Lacking any more precise criteria, one could almost measure the fantastic by the *degree of consciousness* of the heroes on one side, and on the other the *intensity of the dream-images* that surround them." Levy, *Lovecraft,* 13.
114 Kant, *The Critique of Judgment,* 122 and 119.

That was all. After that Johansen only brooded over the idol in his cabin and attended to a few matters for food for himself and the laughing maniac by his side. He did not try to navigate after the first bold flight, for the reaction [of witnessing the colossus that is Cthulhu] had taken something out of his soul. Then came the storm of April 2nd, and a gathering of the clouds about his consciousness. There is a sense of spectral whirling through liquid gulfs of infinity, of dizzying rides through reeling universes on a comet's tail, and of hysterical plunges from the pit to the moon and from the moon back again to the pit, all livened by a cachinnating chorus of the distorted, hilarious elder gods and the green, bat-winged mocking imps of Tartarus.[115]

In this sense, we may consider the Lovecraftian text as a quintessential parody of both Kantian metaphysics and Kantian aesthetics: although the text clearly relies upon the strategic deployment of the unities of synthesis — the Lovecraftian protagonist is the veritable signifier of pure reason[116] — the irreversible plunge of the narrator into either madness or suicidal despair works to ultimately frustrate the supremely humanistic objective of the Kantian theory of the sublime, which is the validation of the anthropocentric through the ultimately successful epistemic subjugation of the inhuman magnitude.[117] Eternally barred from Kantian transcendence, Lovecraft's fictional stand-ins are the apotheosis of *abjection,* defined by Julia Kristeva as existence "at the border of my condition as a living being [...] when [the

---

115 Lovecraft, "The Call of Cthulhu," 156.
116 Harman collectively refers to them as "hardboiled rationalists," which suggests a correlation with the hard-boiled detective that I want to explore in the final chapter. Harman, *Weird Realism,* 69.
117 See also Kant, *The Critique of Judgment,* 125–26: "[T]he irresistibility of [Nature's] might, while making us recognize our own [physical] impotence, considered as beings of nature, discloses to us a faculty of judging independently of, and a superiority over, nature; on which is based a kind of self-preservation, entirely different from that which can be attacked and brought into danger by external nature." For Kant's account of the "positive" sublime, see below.

'I'] finds that the impossible constitutes its very *being* that it *is* none other than the abject."[118] I strongly agree with the argument put forward by Vivian Ralickas: the irredeemably abject condition of Lovecraft's protagonists refutes Will's hypothesis of Lovecraft's subscription to the Kantian notion of the sublime. In my opinion, however, Lovecraft's narrative deployment of the conceit of synthetic unity, albeit in a vulgar form, for purposes of achieving dramatic effect, constitutes a technical *appropriation* of the Kantian imaginary — even if only for the subversive purpose of parody.[119] For what is wholly missing from Lovecraft is any acknowledgment of Kant's notion of the "positive" sublime,[120] the sensation of aesthetic pleasure incurred through the Subject's (meta-)physical overcoming of the sublime object by subordinating it to the intellectual category of the *concept*; the "concept of an Object in general can be immediately combined with the perception of an object, combining its empirical predicates [e.g., magnitude], so as to form a cognitive judgment; and it is thus that a judgment of experience is produced."[121] This is a

118 Kristeva, *Powers of Horror*, 3 and 5. For centrality of the abject to contemporary horror literature and cinema, see Cardin, "George Romero's Living Dead Films as Contemplative Tools," in Cardin, *Dark Awakenings*, 241–86. As Cardin convincingly argues, the seminal conceit of horror following Romero's break-through film *Night of the Living Dead* (1968) is that the traditionally xenophobic "There's something out there" has been supplanted by the contemporarily de-centering "There's something inside me." The revelation of the un-grounded nature of the self is the quintessential abject, meaning that at present the horror film is wholly Lovecraftian in nature, its two dominant concerns — serial murder ("the slasher film") and cannibalism ("the meat movie"; "the zombie picture") lurid filmic displays of abjection.
119 Ralickas, "Cosmic Horror."
120 The Kantian sublime is a two-fold, or dualistic, sensation: "[T]his feeling consists of two contradictory sensations, pleasure and displeasure, 'attraction' and repulsion." Lyotard, *Lessons on the Analytic*, 109.
121 Kant, *The Critique of Judgment*, 162. Hence, the "paradox" of the sublime as aesthetic judgment: "[T]he imagination does not contribute to pleasure through a free production of forms and aesthetic Ideas, but in its powerlessness to give form to the object." Lyotard, *Lessons on the Analytic*, 99. See also ibid., 139–40: "Sublime feeling is aesthetic and, as such, only interests, among the powers of thought, the power of feeling pleasure or displeasure."

form of pleasure and, therefore, an aesthetic sensation properly so called. What Kant identifies as "the regulative Idea of a finality of nature" serves, in the words of Jean-François Lyotard, "to introduce a validation of natural teleology,"[122] precisely because the universality of the principle of judgment is itself "the principle of a teleology of nature for freedom"[123] — the monstrous object might physically kill us, but we shall die as rationally and morally autonomous agents, which proves our ontological superiority to the Thing. Or, more precisely — mind is capable of recognizing that *monstrum* is the true cause of our subjective feeling of the sublime which by itself re-assimilates the Thing into the "absolute of causality"; "What matters in the formulation of sublime feeling is the sensation that there is a cause to be fearful, a terror that corresponds to 'this is frightening,' that is, to a reflective judgment."[124] Man can never be de-centered by nature, but "because there is in our Imagination a striving towards infinite progress, and in our Reason a claim for absolute totality, regarded as a real Idea, therefore this very inadequateness for that Idea in our faculty for estimating the magnitude of things of sense, excites in us the feeling of a supersensible faculty."[125] In the Kantian view, "Great" Cthulhu should not truly frighten us if for no other reason than we can truly know him for what he is — a *monstrum,* which can be reduced by the mind to nothing more than an extraordinarily large series of smaller mathematical (or spatial) units.[126] And, by so doing, we are able to prove, literally, that the Thing's sublimity is simply something that exists only in our mind. Hence the reason for Lovecraft's compulsive deployment of the signature phrase "brain-blasting": with the wholesale annihilation of the synthetic *a priori,* the conditional reassertion of the restorative anthropocentrism promised by Kant[127]

---

122 Lyotard, *Lessons on the Analytic,* 1.
123 Ibid., 3.
124 Ibid., 139.
125 Kant, *The Critique of Judgment,* 109–10.
126 Lyotard, *Lessons on the Analytic,* 112.
127 The regulative Idea of the teleological finality of nature — a quintessentially anti-Lovecraftian concept — serves as the sought-after "bridge" between the

can be eternally preempted.[128] In an equally unconditional manner, Lovecraft repudiates Burke's more visceral version of the positive sublime, which induces a rehabilitative effect on both body and mind.

> Melancholy, dejection, despair, and often self-murder is the consequence of the gloomy view we take of things in [the] relaxed state of the body. The best remedy for all these evils is exercise or labor; and *labor* is a surmounting of *difficulties,* an exertion of the contracting power of the muscles; and as such resembles pain, which consists in tension or contraction, in everything but degree. Labor is not only requisite to preserve the coarser organs in a state fit for their functions, but it is equally necessary to these finer and more delicate organs, on which, and by which, the imagination, and perhaps the other mental powers act.[129]

Terror serves as a precondition for a type of exercise, the exertion of somatic and psychic functions harmonized through the overcoming, either in fact or in imagination, of danger.

> Now, as a due exercise is essential to the coarse muscular parts of the constitution, and that without this routinizing they would become languid, and diseased, the very same rule holds with regard to those finer parts we have mentioned; to

---

theoretical and the practical, "spanning the gulf previously created between the objects of knowledge according to the conditions of possible experience and the realization of freedom under the unconditional of moral law." Ibid., 1.

[128] In his own reading of Kant, Lyotard has provided a philosophically formal exposition that accords remarkably well with the adolescent but emotionally effective Lovecraftian brain-blasting: the dramatic encounter with the un-nameable object "reveals the degree to which the union of faculties is precarious, almost lost—this is the component of anguish in this feeling. The 'aptitude' for Ideas of reason must be developed in order for this perspective of unity to reemerge from the disaster and, to say it simply, for the sublime feeling [i.e., a proper aesthetic sensation] to be possible." Ibid., 25.

[129] Burke, *A Philosophical Enquiry,* 255. Emphases in the original.

have them in proper order, they must be shaken and worked to a proper degree.¹³⁰

Disease, unfortunately, is the hallmark of inhabiting a landscape of an obliterating cosmic disinterestism. As with Kant, so with Burke; Lovecraft's implacable literary sense must drive him to the uncompromising negation of any potential grounds for the reconciliation of Man with Nature: abjection is the only "sentiment" that Lovecraft can maintain with full artistic consistency. Not surprisingly, then, by the end of the tale, Thurston is clearly in an abject state: "I suppose that only a single mountain-top, the hideous monolith-crowned citadel whereon great Cthulhu was buried, actually emerged from the waters. When I think of the *extent* of all that may be brooding down there I almost wish to kill myself forthwith."¹³¹ Presumably he does so; the story we are reading is taken from the papers of the only recently "late" Francis Wayland Thurston of Boston, his uncle, Professor Angell, having been previously killed during a fatal but clandestine encounter with members of the New Orleans branch of the cult.¹³² The subjective experience of the monstrous has yielded Thurston an abject — that is, incommunicable — sensation of pain and wound.

> I have looked upon all that the universe has to hold of horror, and even the skies of spring and the flowers of summer must ever afterward be poison to me. [...] What has risen may sink, and what has sunk may rise. Loathsomeness waits and dreams in the deep, and decay spreads over the tottering cities of men.¹³³

---

130 Ibid., 256.
131 Lovecraft, "The Call of Cthulhu," 156.
132 Ibid., 145.
133 Ibid., 157.

In other words, both Thurston and Angell have aesthetically migrated from the domain of the para-sublime to that of the wholly grotesque.

4. To the Grotesque:
"The Horror at Red Hook" (1925)

> But that fright was so mixed with wonder and alluring
> grotesqueness that it was almost a pleasant sensation.
> — H.P. Lovecraft

> For by what laws may we specify the lawless?
> — Hugh Kenner

As Fredric Jameson argues in *The Geopolitical Aesthetic: Cinema and Space in the World System* (1992), the fatal flaw of the contemporary conspiratorial imagination lies within its "ambitious program of fantasizing an economic system on the scale of the globe itself."[1] Globalization and parapolitics combine to form what Jameson calls the "geopolitical unconscious," the ultimately Sisyphean effort "to think a system so vast that it cannot be encompassed by the natural and historically developed categories of presentation within which human beings normally orient themselves."[2] Accordingly, the contemporary author of the "conspiratorial text" is caught in both an artistic and epistemic bind. In order to possess relevance the conspiratorial text must "constitute an unconscious, collective effort at trying to figure out where we are and what landscapes and forces confront us in a late twentieth century whose abominations are heightened by

1   Jameson, *The Geopolitical Aesthetic*, 9.
2   Ibid., 3.

their concealment and their bureaucratic impersonality."[3] Yet, such a project is doomed to fail at the outset, for the only artistic tools available to the conspiracy theorist are cognitively inadequate. Conspiracy theory "now attempts to refashion national allegory into a conceptual instrument for grasping our new being in the world,"[4] ignoring the fact that both the national and the human scales of reference are precisely that which have been rendered obsolete through the violent irruption of the parapolitical sublime.

> Yet conspiracy theory (and its garish narrative manifestations) must be seen as a degraded attempt—through the figuration of advanced technology—to think the impossible totality of the contemporary world-system. It is in terms of that enormous and threatening, yet only dimly perceivable [obscure?], other reality of economic and social institutions that, in my opinion, the postmodern sublime can alone be adequately theorized.[5]

While Jameson advocates new forms of techno-literature ("high-tech paranoia"[6]), such as the by now hopelessly passé science-fiction sub-genre of cyberpunk—"the supreme *literary* expression if not of postmodernism, then of late capitalism itself"[7]—as the most suitable cultural vehicle for negotiating the geopolitical unconscious,[8] I believe that the resolution of the

---

3   Ibid.
4   Ibid.
5   Jameson, *Postmodernism*, 38.
6   Ibid., 38.
7   Ibid., 419, fn. 1. Emphasis in the original.
8   "Such [conspiracy] narratives, which first tried to find expression through the generic structure of the spy novel, have only recently crystallized in a new type of science fiction, called cyberpunk, which is fully as much an expression of trans-national corporate realities as it is of global paranoia itself: William Gibson's representational innovations, indeed, mark his work as an exceptional literary realization within a predominantly visual or aural postmodern production." Ibid., 38; see also ibid., 35. Jameson falls prey to the same sort of deterministic technophilia that he broadly criticizes the post-

aesthetic dilemma articulated by Jameson lies within the tropes of cosmic horror, specifically within its primary mechanism of forcing the reader into a confrontation with the ontologically unspeakable that has *already* been reduced to the scale of human perception — the *grotesque*.

If we were to appropriate cosmic horror as a literary genre necessary for the development of a parapolitical aesthetics, then two rhetorical moves become necessary: the conceit of parapolitics as morally evil and the conceit of parapolitics as the politically "weird" — specifically, a "weird" version of the conspiracy narrative. It is surprising to realize the degree to which the narrative devices of the weird tale both anticipate and prefigure the parapolitical analytic.

> Horror writers are reactionaries in general simply because they are particularly, one might even say *professionally,* aware of the existence of Evil. It is somewhat curious that among Lovecraft's numerous disciples none has been struck by this simple fact: the evolution of the modern world has made Lovecraftian phobias ever more present, ever more *alive*.[9]

The "points of contact" between the cosmic horror tale and the episodic disclosures of clandestine reality (or "the hideous truth"[10]) are as numerous as they are labored: the misdirected transmission of encoded information that yields catastrophic results ("The Yellow Sign," by Robert W. Chambers), the acci-

---

modernists for; on the basis of anecdotal evidence, the current dominant paradigms of horror fiction, literary and cinematic, are biological, medical, and their hybrid, biomedical. Also worthy of note is the imprint of feminist-inspired narratives of stalking and serial murder as well as a resurgence in tales of hauntings — a nostalgic reaction, perhaps, to our growing awareness that we really do not possess souls after all. Here, the medium is definitely not the message — information technology is merely a contemporary instance of that terror of boundlessness which ultimately hinges upon the threatened annihilation of a subject both embodied and abject. Everything else is just a gimmick. See Ndalianis, *The Horror Sensorium*, 15–39.

9   Houellebecq, *H.P. Lovecraft*, 116.
10 Mariconda, "Lovecraft's Cosmic Imagery," 206, fn. 4.

dental trespass by civilians into the restricted space of encrypted communication broadcasts ("The Willows," by Algernon Blackwood[11]), the unintentional disclosure of a "black" rendition and mind-control operation through the recovery of repressed memories ("The White People," by Arthur Machen). Yet, it is only with Lovecraft's work that covert agency is poetically reconstituted as a systemic property of parapolitical *Existenz*. And he achieves his singularity of effect through an unexpected grounding of his equally singular aestheticism upon a radically materialistic version of conspiracy theory, founded, in turn, upon an utterly unique mytho-poetic rendering of racial hatred. I wholly agree with Houellebecq that Lovecraft's main claim as a "serious" writer lays with his unrivaled appropriation of the racist imaginary as a literary trope for the production of a metaphysical literature of cosmic horror: "The other great cause of my surprise [when reading Lovecraft] was his obsessive racism. [...] The role of this racial hatred in Lovecraft's work has often been underestimated. [...] [N]ever in the reading of his descriptions of nightmare creatures could I have divined that their source was to be found in *real* human beings."[12] Lovecraft's singular racism proves inseparable from his signature cosmic disinterestism: "Lovecraft has not so much the steady gaze of objective nihilism as the transmogrifying vision of hysterical nihilism, from which his racism is inextricable."[13] Both are manifestations of a post-metaphysical theological/apocalyptic imaginary, highly susceptible to treatment as an aestheticized re-working of conspiracy theory.

---

11   Not coincidentally, this weird tale also contains the greatest piece of "practical advice" for the parapolitical investigator in this era of the global hegemony of the NSA: "There are forces close here that could kill a herd of elephants in a second as easily as you or I could squash a fly. Our only chance is to keep perfectly still. Our insignificance perhaps may save us." Blackwood, "The Willows," 39–40.
12   Houellebecq, *H.P. Lovecraft*, 24 and 108.
13   Mieville, "Introduction," xix.

Here we approach what lies beneath Lovecraft's racism [...]. Already the varnish of civilization was cracking; the forces of Evil await "patient and potent" because they are going to regenerate again on earth. Underlying these ruminations on the decay of cultures, which are merely a superimposed layer of intellectual justification, is fear. Fear from afar, preceded by repulsion — it is what generates indignation and hatred.[14]

Cosmic horror would seem to be the only form of "high art" that racism can possibly take, precisely because a philosophically sophisticated racist aesthetics would have to be grounded upon an anti-Kantian ontology of the monstrous.

The decisive moment in Lovecraft's literary development occurred between March 1924 and April 1926, when he lived in Brooklyn: "The inescapable truth is that Lovecraft's fame lies in only a dozen or so stories written between 1926 and 1935; that only his late fiction contains the elements by which we characteristically refer to his work as *Lovecraftian*."[15] I partially disagree with this assessment; in my opinion, five early tales meet the definition of wholly Lovecraftian, often in novel and unexpected ways: they are "Dagon" (1917), "Nyarlathotep" (1920), "From Beyond" (1920), "The Music of Erich Zann" (1921), and "The Festival" (1923). Nonetheless, it remains indisputable that Lovecraft's time in Gotham proved the pivotal event, which seems to have operated in two ways. The first, as we should expect, was the para-sublime reaction to New York as an architectonic phenomenon — one that suspiciously resembles Lovecraft's compelling description of the "impossible" sunken city of R'lyeh. New York is the nameless place "where the verticality of the skyscraper is only an exterior dimension! Instead of being rooted in the earth, these dwellings spurt out vertiginously toward the sky. This is a place devoid of a centre or an identity or ties with the past, a city to which none of the many ethnic groups composing it

---

14 Houellebecq, *H.P. Lovecraft*, 113.
15 Schultz, "From Microcosm to Macrocosm," 208–9.

really belong."[16] Or, as Lovecraft revealingly put it in one of his "New York tales," "He" (1925), in the "Cyclopean [!] modern towers and pinnacles that rise blackly Babylonian under waning moons, I had found instead only a sense of horror and oppression which threatened to master, paralyse, and annihilate me."[17] Houellebecq insightfully comments upon the masochistic nature of Lovecraft's New York writings; the focus is monomaniacally upon the abject reduction of the protagonist as the impotent victim of a cosmic conspiracy whose sign is the monstrous template of a diabolical landscape of inhuman architecture. "His descriptions of the nightmare entities that populate the Cthulhu cycle spring directly from this hallucinatory vision,"[18] the outpourings, according to Levy, of a "pitiable paranoiac, the plaything of cosmic forces."[19]

> For full three seconds I could glimpse that pan-daemonic sight, and in those seconds I saw a vista which will ever afterward torment me in dreams. I saw the heavens verminous with strange flying things, and beneath them a hellish black city of giant stone terraces with impious pyramids flung savagely to the moon, and devil-lights burning from unencumbered windows. And swarming loathsomely on aerial galleries, I saw the yellow, squint-eyed people of that

---

16 Levy, *Lovecraft*, 36. "Space is a discursive practice of a place. A place is a given area, named and mapped, that can be measured in terms of surface and volume. It becomes space only when it becomes a site of existential engagement among living agents who mark it with their activities or affiliate with dialogue and active perception." Conley, "Space," 258. In a letter of Lovecraft to his friend Donald Wandrei dated 10 February, 1927, he writes: "New York [...] has no central identity or meaning, & no clear-cut relationship either to its own past or to anything in particular." Levy, *Lovecraft*, 127, fn. 3.
17 Lovecraft, "He," 119.
18 Houellebecq, *H.P. Lovecraft*, 107.
19 Levy, *Lovecraft*, 169. For Airaksinen, masochism is the libidinal foundation of Lovecraft's singular literary style of "un-writing": "[a]ll the monsters, and their projections, are based on the simple experience at the root of Lovecraftian horror, namely, the disappearance of our identity." Airaksinen, *The Philosophy of H.P. Lovecraft*, 101.

city, robed horribly in orange and red, and dancing insanely to the pounding of fevered kettle-drums, and the clatter of obscene crotala, and the maniacal moaning of muted horns whose ceaseless dirges rose and fell undulantly like the waves of an unhallowed ocean of bitumen.[20]

A prophetic vision of New York after the "success" of the reverse colonization. But this striking passage is made even more remarkable when one realizes that it is only a slightly more rarefied version of a letter that Lovecraft composed conveying his own impressions of the "real time-space" of Brooklyn.

The organic things — Italo-Semitic-Mongoloid — inhabiting that awful cesspool could not by any stretch of the imagination be called human. They were monstrous and nebulous adumbrations of the pithecanthropoid and amoebal; vaguely molded from some stinking viscous slime of earth's corruption, and slithering and oozing in and on the filthy streets or in and out of windows and doorways in a fashion suggestive of nothing but infesting worms or deep-sea unnamabilities. They — or the degenerate gelatinous fermentation of which they were composed — seemed to ooze, seep and trickle through the gaping cracks in the horrible houses... and I thought of some avenue of Cyclopean and unwholesome vats, crammed to the vomiting-point with gangrous vileness, and about to burst and inundate the world in one leprous cataclysm of semi-fluid rottenness. From that nightmare of perverse infection I could carry not away the memory of any living face. The individually grotesque was lost in the collectively devastating; which left on the eye only the broad, phantasmal line`ments of the morbid mould of disintegration and decay... a yellow and leering mask with sour,

20 Lovecraft, "He," 126–27. "'He' was written during the night of August 10–11, 1925, after Lovecraft went on a solitary all-night expedition through various parts of the New York metropolitan area that led him finally to Scott Park in Elizabeth, New Jersey." Joshi, "Explanatory Notes," in Lovecraft, "The Call of Cthulhu," 388.

> sticky, acid ichors oozing at eyes, ears, nose, and mouth, and abnormally bubbling from monstrous and unbelievable sores at every point…[21]

Lovecraft did not like New York City very much, but his (unpleasant) time there proved invaluable to the execution of his greatest literary effect: the dramatic unification of the architectonic with the degenerate — an utterly improbable but narratively effective synthesis of high and low. More precisely,

> New York had marked him forever. During the course of 1925, his hatred of the "foul mongrels" of this modern Babylon, the "foreign colossus that gibbers and howls vulgarly…" did not cease to exasperate him and drove him delirious. It could even be posited that a fundamental figure in his own body of work — the idea of a grand, titanic city, in whose foundations crawl repugnant nightmare beings — sprang directly from his New York experience.[22]

As Levy rightly argues, it is in the Ctulhu Mythos, the essential elements of which were formulated during Lovecraft's sojourn in Brooklyn, "that Lovecraft's tales gain their profound unity."

> Except for some details, all develop the same central theme; all make reference to the same deities; all put on stage the same characters devoted to the same occult practices. Above all, the same images recur under the author's pen with an obsessive insistence, to form a tight web around the mythic

---

21 Levy, *Lovecraft*, 28–29.
22 Houellebecq, *H.P. Lovecraft*, 103. "The myths of Cthulhu draw their cold power from the sadistic delectation with which Lovecraft subjects humans, punished for their resemblance to the New York rabble that had humiliated him, to the persecution of beings come from the stars." Francis Lacassin, editor of the French language edition of Lovecraft's works, cited in ibid., 108–9.

contents of the work, ensuring its cohesion and giving it its consistency.[23]

It is within an unparalleled "nomadic bestiary" of the transversal cross-references and intertextual borrowings infusing Lovecraft's a-theological and apocalyptic imagining[24] that suffice in showing how

> Lovecraft *dreamed his repugnances* and with what verbal richness he ranted from purely sensory data. [...] We thus touch [...] upon the heart of the problem in Lovecraft's fantastic creation, where the hideous monsters are in large part merely the projection, in the "dark chamber" of a sick mind, of obsessive images that his political and racial vision of the American world had given him.[25]

The correct literary term for Lovecraft's rants is the *grotesque*; as Mikhail Bahktin famously observed in his master work on Rabelais and the carnivalesque, "Exaggeration, hyperbolism, excessiveness are generally considered fundamental attributes of the grotesque style."[26] The grotesque, perhaps best defined as "the ambivalently abnormal," is phenomenological in nature, grounded upon a *horror sensorium* of the body: "a fundamentally ambivalent thing, [...] a violent clash of opposites, [...] an appropriate expression of the problematical nature of existence."[27] When treating the grotesque imaginary, as Bakhtin reminds us, we must always "take into consideration the importance of cosmic terror, the fear of the immeasurable, the infinitely powerful."[28] The body is itself the onto-poetical ground of the grotesque, a body that is eternally teetering on the verge of a chaotic formlessness through the radical and uncontrol-

---

23 Levy, *Lovecraft*, 109; see also 84.
24 Ibid., 26–30 and 79–85.
25 Ibid., 29.
26 Bakhtin, *Rabelais and His World,* 303 and Chapter Five, 303–67.
27 Thomson, *The Grotesque,* 11.
28 Bakhtin, *Rabelais and His World,* 335.

lable proliferation of irreconcilable combinations, the perpetual construction of "what we might call a double body"[29]: "The grotesque body [...] is a body in the act of becoming. It is never finished, never completed; it is continually built, created, and builds and creates another body."[30]

Like the sublime, then, the grotesque is quintessentially modern, but with this crucial distinction: both modernism and the grotesque "focus on the concepts of alienation, subjectivity, and absurdity, but the grotesque tends to focus on explicit representations of these ideas through disturbing imagery and actions, while modernism tends to focus on more implicit representations of these themes."[31] In other words, the aesthetic paradigm of the grotesque requires the coming forth of a monster of some kind;[32] the "grotesque alienation" that results arises from an enhanced self-consciousness of the protagonist of being embedded within a pre-existent (un-constructed) estranged world/parapolitical landscape: the dark numinous.[33] Undertaking the most ambitious analysis of the grotesque as a formal sub-category of the modern, Wolfgang Kayser defines his subject matter in such a way as to render most transparent the artistic and narrative similitudes between the grotesque and cosmic horror: "The modern age questions the validity of the anthropological and the relevance of the scientific concepts un-

---

29 Ibid., 318.
30 Ibid., 317.
31 Martin, *H.P. Lovecraft*, 47.
32 "Grotesque alienation is usually a result of external, physical change or action, communicated through imagery that may include violent acts, self-destructive behaviors [*sic*], deformity, transformation, monstrous creatures, and any number of other strange or disturbing scenes. However, the physically-based alienation depicted in such works is merely a catalyst or metaphor for the psychological alienation of one or more characters." Ibid., 48–49.
33 "In modernist grotesque alienation, there is no going back. The world is not alienated due to malignant influences that can be purged, as in the older [classical?] grotesque. In modernist grotesque alienation, the protagonist realizes that the world itself has always been alienating, and it is the illusion of stability that must be exposed, for the sake of intellectual integrity." Ibid., 51.

derlying the syntheses of the nineteenth century. The various forms of the grotesque are the most obvious and pronounced contradictions of any kind of rationalism and any systematic use of thought."[34] (In Kantian terms, we would say that the grotesque is suspended between the absence of meaning and the un-decidability of meaning.) This is wholly consistent with the grotesque's notoriously difficult-to-pin-down role in the history of art. Although the style first emerged in 15th-century Italy, the *grottesche* ("of the underground"[35]) long served as nothing more than a highly suspect form of ornamentalism, but one that carried with it a powerful metaphysical punch: the unbridled proliferation of hybrid images[36] in the empty spaces or margins of frescoes and manuscripts alike afforded a radical de-structuring of the central text (or image) of the allegedly "serious" work of art immediately juxtaposed to it. In this way, the monstrous was reconstituted as a rival system of meaning, or subtext, to the ostensibly non-monstrous imaginary of the text: "with the advent of human-animal figures, ornament was beginning to present a potential rival to the central message, a competing text."[37] As Harpham has powerfully argued, the "problem of the relation between center and border is raised in miniature by this [grotesque] figure — which is within which: which is the dominant principle and which the subordinate element?"[38] The impossible hybrids of the *grottesche* signify a radical reversibility be-

---

34 Kayser, *The Grotesque in Art and Literature*, 188.
35 Unforgettably savaged by the Roman architect Vitrivius thusly: "In the stucco are monsters rather than definitive representations taken from definite things [...]. Such things neither are, nor can be, nor have been." Cited in Harpham, *On the Grotesque*, 26. The invention — or recovery — of grotesque art was occasioned by the excavation of the *Domus Aurea* (Golden Palace) of Nero in Rome around 1480. See ibid., 23–47.
36 As Harpham remarks, "Grotesque forms place an enormous strain on the marriage of form and content by foregrounding them both, so that they appear not as a partnership, but as a warfare, a struggle." Ibid., 7.
37 Ibid., 34–35.
38 Ibid., 35. As a result, "All grotesque Art threatens the notion of a center by implying coherencies just out of reach, metaphors or analogies just beyond our reach." Ibid., 43.

tween monstrous and non-monstrous realities, a "paralysis of language"[39] which is the condition of the uncanny: "When an absence of meaning is created by unprecedented strangeness, so that we know that our experience has not adequately prepared us to interpret or read the design, the ornament not only soothes, but stimulates as well."[40] The grotesque is nothing more than Otto's daemonic–divine in decorative form. If the monster is The-Thing-That-Should-Not-Be, then the grotesque is The-Image-That-Should-Not-Be-Made,[41] bearing within it the primal duality and sacred pollution of the holy. I would go so far as to argue that grotesque art was Western civilization's way of making the *abject aesthetically permissible*; modernity's artistic privileging of the grotesque/abject is itself decisive confirmation that, following romanticism, the center does not hold — or that the "marginal" prevails.

For Kayser, the grotesque consists of three signature themes, all of them daemonic. The first is "the grotesque as the estranged world": "It is our world which has to be transformed. Suddenness and surprise are essential elements of the grotesque."[42] The grotesque "world," or landscape, as Bakhtin makes clear, is the aesthetic continuation by other means of the phenomenological primacy of the grotesque body.

> Thus the artistic logic of the grotesque image ignores the closed, smooth, and the impenetrable surface of the body and retains only its excrescences (sprouts, buds) and orifices, only that which leads beyond the body's limited space or into the body's depths. Mountains and abysses, such is the relief of the grotesque body; or speaking in architectural terms, tow-

---

39 Ibid., 6. In the alternative, "If the grotesque can be compared to anything, it is to paradox." Ibid., 19.
40 Ibid., 33.
41 "Grotesque figures test us […] for they seem to be singular events, appearing in the world by virtue of an illegitimate act of creation, manifesting no coherent, and certainly no divine, intention." Ibid., 5. In other words — blasphemous.
42 Kayser, *The Grotesque in Art and Literature*, 184.

ers and subterranean passages. [...] This grotesque logic is also extended to images of nature and of objects in which depends (holes) and convexities are emphasized.[43]

The "estranged world" of the grotesque, unifying both the high and the low, is, therefore, an artistic device deployed primarily in order to stage the mimetic rendition of the trauma-inducing encounter with the radically alien "sublime." The grotesque "is primarily the expression of our failure to orient ourselves in the physical universe [...]. We are so strongly affected and terrified because it is our world which ceases to be reliable, and we feel unable to live in this changed world"[44]: in short, Scott contemplating the "truth" of American history after 9/11. But not only Scott; Lovecraft as well.

> The grotesque instills fear of life rather than fear of death.[45] Structurally, it presupposes that the categories which apply to our world view become inapplicable[;] [...] the fusion of realms which we know to be separated, the abolition of the law of statics, the loss of identity, the distortion of "natural" size and shape, the suspension of the category of objects, the destruction of personality, and the fragmentation of the historical order.[46]

Second is what Kayser denotes as "the Grotesque as a Play with the Absurd," signified by the operational hegemony of determinism (natural or otherwise) and the concomitant manipulation of reality by occult forces: "the unity of perspective in the grotesque consists in an unimpassioned view of life on earth as an empty, meaningless puppet play or a caricatural marionette

---

43 Bakhtin, *Rabelais and His World*, 317–18; 318, fn. 6.
44 Ibid.
45 The existential situation of Thurston at the conclusion of "The Call of Cthulhu."
46 Kayser, *The Grotesque in Art and Literature*, 184–85.

theatre."[47] And third is the rather convoluted "the Grotesque as an Attempt to Invoke and Subdue the Demonic Aspects of the World," which may perhaps best be defined in the following manner: "In spite of all the helplessness and horror inspired by the dark forces which lurk in and behind our world and have the power to estrange it, the truly artistic portrayal effects a secret liberation. The darkness has been sighted, the ominous powers discovered, the incomprehensible forces challenged."[48]

The applicability of Kayser's theory of the grotesque to Lovecraft's cosmic horror should be obvious, although it is necessary to slightly qualify the performative function of "exorcism." While Kayser faintly echoes the classic trope of the heroic, both Lovecraftian landscape[49] and narrative signal nothing more clearly than decadence: "Decrepitude, corruption settle wherever the supernatural has intruded. The Lovecraftian fantastic is manifestly *decadent*: The bizarre does not fall from space to terrify or confound, but to corrupt.[50] It is a type of gangrene that gnaws,

---

47 Ibid., 186. For the intimate connections between the grotesque and caricature, see Thomson, *The Grotesque*, 38–40. Striking here is the utter aptness of the marionette theater as the signifier of the Deep State.
48 Kayser, *The Grotesque in Art and Literature*, 188.
49 As made clear in such seminal tales as "The Color Out of Space," Lovecraft's "blasted heath" is "not so much a physical phenomenon as a psychological process, a fear-response and an awe, in a mind that by the very experience discovers its own minuteness and precariousness in a cosmos far vaster, far more indifferent to human concerns than that mind has ever imagined." Martin, *H.P. Lovecraft*, 175. According to Levy, "It is well known that the truly fantastic exists only where the impossible can make an irruption, through time and space, into an objectively familiar locale. [...] These imaginary places form, in the real topography of New England, a zone of shadow, a zone of mystery, a dream-zone, which spreads little by little to the rest of the countryside, contaminating the diurnal space of the maps and charts and giving it a suddenly different aspect. [...] Arkham is, in the most precise sense of the term, a structure condensed from dreams, around which is built and organized an entire universe of inexpressible wonders and blasphemous horrors. Arkham and its vicinity are, in the Lovecraftian topography, the fault through which the bizarre, the horrific, the disquieting, the morbid, and the unclean spread." Levy, *Lovecraft*, 36–37. In short, Lovecraft's topography is parapolitical.
50 Lovecraft, "The Colour Out of Space."

wears away, and finally rots the familiar world through and through,"[51] with the result that "[p]erspective itself is distorted."[52] Not surprisingly, the "world depicted by the grotesque artist is our own world turned upside down; our standards, conventions, convictions are upset."[53] Nevertheless, Lovecraft's weird tale does manage to effect a kind of an exorcism of its own, one, we should come to expect, that is infused with parapolitical implication: R'lyeh re-surfaces and then re-submerges *while waiting to re-surface again*. Not the least of Lovecraft's literary innovations is that he managed to successfully obviate the central dramatic impediment of the science fiction tale of alien invasion (or reverse colonization): how can mere humanity possibly defeat an alien civilization possessing super-advanced technology (or hyper-atavistic primitivism)? Lovecraft's ingenious solution lies with his singular utilization of anti-Kantian cosmic measurements of time — the "invasion" is not defeated, but indefinitely delayed; the decadent un-hero learns the truth and perceives the alien menace (dark *alētheia*) but survives through the fortuitousness of the not-quite-yet-completed winding down of the cosmic clock.[54] This, of course, broadly corresponds to the defining "triple rhythm" of both the Gothic tale and the race fantasy of reverse colonization: "the monster appears, the monster terrifies, the monster is expelled."[55] Even more revealing is the manner in which the grotesque tale directly imitates the more encompassing narrative structure of the Gothic tale, which "first invites or admits a monster, then entertains or is entertained by monstrosity for some extended duration, until in its closing pages it expels or repudiates the monster and all the disruption that he/she/it brings." No less an authority than Abdhul Al-Hazred himself declares in his darkly magisterial *Necronomicon* that "Man rules now where They ruled once; They shall

51 Levy, *Lovecraft*, 38.
52 Ibid., 37. As a "cosmic conspiracist," perhaps Lovecraft's most obvious counterpart is Thomas Pynchon. See Meikle, "Other Frequencies."
53 Clayborough, *The Grotesque in English Literature*, 71.
54 Christopher Craft, cited in Arata, "The Occidental Tourist," 641.
55 Wisnicki, *Conspiracy, Revolution, and Terrorism*, 173.

soon rule where Man rules now. After summer is winter, and after winter summer. They wait patient and potent, for here shall they reign again."[56] First and foremost, Lovecraft was a Spenglerian.[57] Predictably, Lovecraft identifies race conspiracy as the primary degenerative factor governing the death of civilizations: "The supreme calamity of the western world…was the rashly and idealistically admitted flood of alien, degenerate, and unassimilable immigrants…Its first results we behold today, through the depths of its cultural darkness are reserved for the torture of later generations."[58]

"The Horror at Red Hook" (August 1925), perhaps the first of Lovecraft's New York tales, is exemplary in the manner in which it unites both the grotesque body and grotesque space into a single narrative device for the re-staging of the race conspiracy theory of reverse colonization. Readers who are already familiar with Lovecraft may wonder why I have not chosen to base my discussion on the late tale of "The Shadow over Innsmouth," published in 1931 and arguably Lovecraft's most spectacular foray into the grotesque.[59] Although I discuss "The Shadow over Innsmouth" in the conclusion, my main reason for affording priority to the artistically inferior "Horror at Red Hook" is the centrality of the New York connection: it is Lovecraft's grotesque re-imaginings of Brooklyn as a landscape of both cosmic horror and race conspiracy that is essential not only to the development of Lovecraft's own work but also to the relevance of his oeuvre to the development of a parapolitical aesthetic. Essentially devoid of a plot, the text is a series of paranoid and increasingly phantasmagorical vignettes in which the illegal immigrant and alien

---

56 Lovecraft, "The Dunwich Horror," 220.
57 Mieville, "Introduction," xix. See also Joshi, *H.P. Lovecraft: The Decline of the West*, 133–45.
58 Lovecraft, cited in Joshi, *H.P. Lovecraft: The Decline of the West*, 137.
59 "Are we not told, in the *Necronomicon*, that the Old Ones exist 'not in the spaces we know, but *between* them?' And did not Lovecraft, by 1931, evolve an aesthetic of weird fiction that exactly embodied this conception?" Joshi, "Introduction," Lovecraft, *The Thing on the Doorstep*, xv. For the virulently eugenic subtext of the tale, see Lovett-Graff, "Shadows over Lovecraft."

conspirator is reduced to a free-floating signifier of a nameless but *globalized* grotesquerie.

> Daily life had for him come to be a phantasmagoria of macabre shadow-studies; now glittering and leering with concealed rottenness as in Beardsley's best manner, now hinting terrors behind the commonest shapes and objects as in the subtler and less obvious works of Gustave Doré. He would often regard it as merciful that most persons of high intelligence jeer at the innermost mysteries; for, he argued, if superior minds were ever placed in fullest contact with the secrets preserved by ancient and lowly cults, the resultant abnormalities would soon not only wreck the work, but threaten the very integrity of the universe.[60]

In essence a detective story, although not a camouflaged one as in the case of "The Call of Cthulhu," "The Horror of Red Hook" is noteworthy in two ways. The first is the complete synthesis of the grotesque space with the alien body, yielding a landscape that is in equal portions both absurd and conspiratorial.

> And now, as he reviewed the things he had seen and felt and apprehended, Malone was content to keep unshared the secret of what could reduce a dauntless fighter to a quivering neurotic; what could make old brick slums and seas of dark, subtle faces a thing of nightmare and eldritch portent. [...] [F]or was not his very act of plunging into the polyglot abyss of New York's underworld a freak beyond sensible explanation? What could he tell the prosaic of the antique witcheries and grotesque marvels discernible to sensitive eyes amidst the poison cauldron where all the varied dregs of unwholesome ages mix their venom and perpetuate their obscene terrors? He had seen the hellish green flame of secret wonder in this blatant, evasive welter of outward greed and inward

60 Lovecraft, "The Horror at Red Hook," 127–28.

blasphemy, and had smiled gently when all the New-Yorkers he knew scoffed at his experiment in police work.[61]

The second is the absolute distinction between perception and reality, a re-deployment in a popular manner of Schopenhauer's post-Kantian formulation of the binary relationship between the noumenal and the phenomenal.

> [Malone] was conscious, as one who united imagination with scientific knowledge, that modern people under lawless conditions tend uncannily to repeat the darkest instinctive patterns of primitive half-ape savagery in their daily life and ritual observances; and he often viewed with an anthropologist's shudder the chanting, cursing processions of bleareyed and pockmarked young men which wound their way along in the small hours of morning. […] They chilled and fascinated him more than he dared confess to his associates on the force, for he seemed to see in them some monstrous thread of secret continuity; some fiendish, cryptical, and ancient pattern utterly beyond and below the sordid mass of facts and habits and haunts listed with such conscientious technical care by the police. They must be, he felt inwardly, the heirs of some shocking and primordial tradition; the shares of debased and broken scraps from cults and ceremonies older than mankind. Their coherence and definiteness suggested it, and it shewed in the singular suspicion of order which lurked beneath their squalid disorder.[62]

Consistent with Lovecraft's a-holy numinous, the element of the grotesque, both as body and as Boschean landscape, are both recast in a materialist form, with both the eugenic theory of racial degeneration and the reactionary's paranoia of reverse colonization serving as the vehicles of translation. The pock-marked sub-humans of Red Hook are narratively appropriated by Love-

61 Ibid., 127.
62 Ibid., 129–30.

craft as the non-Caucasian denizens of what was to become the Cthulhu cult of the later Mythos; here, the so-called "plot" concerns the resurrection of a Kurdish/Zoroastrian "devil-worshipping" cult[63] — an unsolicited "cultural import" from the Middle East.

> [Robert] Suydam's new associates were among the blackest and most vicious criminals of Red Hook's devious lanes, and that at least a third of them were known and repeated offenders in the matter of thievery, disorder, and the importation of illegal immigrants. Indeed, it would not have been too much to say that the old scholar's particular circle coincided almost perfectly with the worst of the organized cliques which smuggled ashore certain nameless and unclassified Asian dregs wisely turned back by Ellis Island. [...] They had come in steamships, apparently tramp freighters, and had been unloaded by stealth on moonless nights in rowboats which stole under a certain wharf and followed a hidden canal to a secret subterranean pool beneath a house.[64]

The topography of the narrative is the grotesque space reworked as metropolitan desolation: the "grotesque" body of New York perforated by the channels of invasion and clandestine penetration; in this case, "underground" people-smuggling networks, which are merely the narrative pretext for the "true" horror of the demonic/immigrant slum — miscegenation.

> Suydam was evidently a leader in extensive man-smuggling operations, for the canal to his house was but one of several

---

63 It is interesting to note that throughout the tale Lovecraft explicitly references his earlier paradigmatic text, "The Music of Erich Zann": "All at once, from an arcaded avenue leading endlessly away, there came the daemonic rattle and wheeze of a blasphemous organ, choking and rumbling out the mockeries of hell in a cracked, sardonic bass. [...] The strange dark men [Kurds] danced in the rear, and the whole column skipped and leaped with Dionysiac fury." Ibid., 142.

64 Ibid., 132 and 133.

> subterranean channels and tunnels in the neighborhood. There was a tunnel from this house to a crypt beneath the dance-hall church[65]; a crypt accessible from the church only through a narrow secret passage in the north wall, and in whose chambers some singular and terrible things were discovered[,] [...] including four mothers with infants of disturbingly strange appearance. These infants died soon after exposure to the light; a circumstance which the doctors thought rather merciful.[66]

Consistent with the meta-narrative pattern of reverse colonization, which is itself the racist expression of the anterior form of the gothic tale, the monster is encountered, endured, and finally defeated. But this time in strictly Lovecraftian terms; the middle sequence of "the monster terrifies" is presented as the brain-blasting trauma of epistemic rupture.

> Avenues of limitless night seemed to radiate in every direction, till one might fancy that here lay the root of the contagion destined to sicken and swallow cities, and engulf nations in the foeter of hybrid pestilence. Here cosmic sin had entered, and festered by an unhallowed rites had commenced the grinning march of death that was to rot us all to fungous abnormalities too hideous for the grave's holding. [...] The world and Nature were helpless against such assaults from unsealed wells of night, nor could any sign or prayer check the Walpurgis-riot of horror which had come when a sage with a hateful key had stumbled on a horde with the locked and brimming coffer of transmitted daemon-lore.[67]

In a similar manner, the "exorcism," or "the monster is expelled," sequence is staged as both a critique of Kant and as a re-affirmation of racist paranoia. The irreducible diversity of the noume-

---

65 Described as "nominally Catholic." Ibid., 132.
66 Ibid., 144.
67 Ibid., 141.

nal realm is safely "exorcised" through the arbitrary reassertion of *ratio* and "human measure."

> *Of course it was a dream* […]. But at the time it was all horribly real, and nothing can ever efface the memory of those knighted crypts, those titan arcades, and those half-formed shapes of hell that strode gigantically in silence holding half-eaten things whose still surviving portions screamed for mercy or laughed with madness.[68]

Secondly, the attempted reverse colonization is defeated by means of a displacement that moves toward future time — within a Spenglerian world-history, decay and downfall are inevitable, although the apocalypse may be preempted by means of surveillance and intervention.

> The soul of the beast is omnipresent and triumphant, and Red Hook's legions of blear-eyed, pockmarked youths still chant and curse and howl as they file from abyss to abyss, none knows whence or whither, pushed on by blind laws of biology which they may never understand. As of old, more people enter Red Hook than leave it on the landward side, and there are already rumors of new canals running underground to certain centers of traffic in liquor and less mentionable things.[69]

An expressly parapolitical reading of "The Horror at Red Hook" should be easy to make out. The subversive "affect" of the text ultimately relies upon the dual reading — one biological, the other political — that the hybridity of monstrosity, represented as racial degeneration, permits. For Levy,

> It is […] useful to say that a monster is not *by nature* fantastic. It becomes truly so only if it manifests itself outside

---

68 Ibid., 140. Emphasis added.
69 Ibid., 145.

all systems and all doctrines. Animated with a perverse autonomy, it must assert itself in total freedom. [...] [Monsters] are characterized above all by their hybridism — a hybridism that is not the simple juxtaposition of disparate elements as in some monsters of antiquity, but as a result of a sort of contamination or collective pollution.[70]

The "monsters" of Red Hook themselves, therefore, "are not the objects of fear, but rather the paradigm crisis that they symbolize"[71]: alterity. More specifically, the alterity of the monsters and what they signify "is raised to the extreme degree by a systematic emphasis on its complete and utter incompatibility with anything known by means of the senses or reason, understandable by logic, or expressible in discursive language."[72] The issue of the tactile sensibility, or the crypto-materialism of the grotesque (as opposed to the always immeasurable magnitude of the sublime), is essential for the aesthetic effect of cosmic horror. In Lovecraft's own words,

It may be well to remark [...] that occult believers are probably less effective than materialists in delineating the spectral and the fantastic, since to them the phantom world is so commonplace a reality that they tend to refer to it with less awe, remoteness, and impressiveness than do those who see in it an absolute and stupendous violation of the natural order.[73]

As Houellebecq has once again rightly noted, "Howard Phillips Lovecraft was not a theoretician[;] [...] by introducing materialism into the heart of fear and fantasy, HPL created a new genre. [...] There exists no horror less psychological, less *debatable*."[74] It is this critical highlighting of bodily horror, or *horror sensori-*

70 Levy, *Lovecraft*, 56.
71 Martin, *H.P. Lovecraft*, 178.
72 Hanegraaff, "Fiction in the Desert of the Real," 99.
73 Lovecraft, "Supernatural," 154–55.
74 Houellebecq, *H.P. Lovecraft*, 46.

um, which enables Lovecraft's singular appropriation of the phenomenological aspect of the grotesque: "Lovecraft's rationalistic intellect could conceive no weirder or more bizarre happening than a dislocation of natural law. […] Being a materialist, Lovecraft created the *materialistic tale of supernatural horror.*"[75] There is considerable debate within Lovecraft scholarship as to the exact nature and role played by the "supernatural" within the Cthulhu Mythos. Although nearly all of Lovecraft's classic early texts are clearly within the supernatural vein, such as "The Outsider" (1921) and "The Festival," many of the tales of the Mythos, including "The Whisperer in Darkness" and "The Shadow Out of Time," seek to provide a crypto-scientific "explanation" of the Old Ones by classifying them as extra-terrestrials. My own feeling is that the issue can best be resolved by holding to one of the central conceits of the Mythos that what is conventionally denoted as "black magic" is really a highly encoded form of a radically alternative physics. Hence the extreme, and grotesquely repulsive, materiality of Cthulhu at the shrieking climax of the seminal text: the fleeing seamen, desperate to escape the pursuing anti-god, turn their own vessel against "him(?)," using it as a projectile.

> Slowly, amidst the distorted horrors of that indescribable scene, [the vessel *Alert*] began to churn the lethal waters; whilst on the masonry of that charnel shore that was not of earth the titan Thing from the stars slavered and gibbered like Polypheme cursing the fleeing ship of Odysseus. Then, bolder than the storied Cyclops, great Cthulhu slid greasily into the water and began to pursue with vast wave-raising strokes of cosmic potency. […] There was a mighty eddying and foaming in the noisome brine, and as the steam mounted higher and higher the brave Norwegian drove his vessel head on against the pursuing jelly which rose above the unclean froth like the stern of a daemon galleon. The awful squid-head with writhing feelers came nearly up to the bowsprit of

75 Berruti, 408, fn. 41.

the sturdy yacht, but Johansen drove on relentlessly. There was a bursting as of an exploding bladder, a slushy nastiness as of a cloven sunfish, a stench as of a thousand opened graves, and a sound that the chronicler could not put on paper. For an instant the ship was befouled by an acrid and blinding green cloud, and then there was only a venomous seething astern; where — God in heaven! — the scattered plasticity of that nameless sky-spawn was nebulously *recombining* in its hateful original form, while its distance widened every second as the *Alert* gained impetus from its mounting steam.[76]

Even more audacious is the descent into full-blown pseudoscience in the late masterpiece "At the Mountains of Madness" (1931) which features, among other things, the content of a medical autopsy of the remains of a deceased Elder One.

Important discovery. [...] Arrangements reminds one of certain monsters of primal myth, especially fabled Elder Things in *Necronomicon*. [...] Objects are eight feet long all over. Six-foot five-ridged barrel torso 3.5 feet central diameter, 1 foot end diameters. Dark grey, flexible, and infinitely tough. Seven-foot membraneous wings of same colour, found folded, spread out furrows between ridges.[77] Wing framework tubular or glandular, of lighter grey, with orifices as wing

---

76 Lovecraft, "The Call of Cthulhu," 155 and 156.
77 See Kayser on the flying rodent as a signifier of the grotesque. "The grotesque animal incarnate [...] is the bat [...] the very name of which points to an unnatural fusion of organic realms concretized in this ghostly creature. And strange habits complement its strange appearance. An animal of the dusk, the bat flies noiselessly, has exceedingly subtle senses, and moves so rapidly that one could easily suspect it of sucking the blood of sleeping animals. It is strange even in the state of repose when its wings cover it like a coat and it hangs, head down, from a rafter, more like a piece of dead matter than a living thing." Kayser, *The Grotesque in Art and Literature*, 183. One of the most unique, and uncanny, characteristics of the Old Ones is that they undertake their periodic interstellar migrations by means of winged flight — vast waves of Goya-esque bat-like aliens flapping through the absolute darkness of the cosmic abyss is an image not readily dismissed.

tips. Spread wings have serrated edges. Around equator, one at central apex of each of the five vertical, stave-like ridges, are five systems of light grey flexible arms or tentacles found tightly folded to torso but expansible to maximum length of over 3 feet. Like arms of primitive crinoid. Single stalks 3 inches diameter branch after 6 inches into five sub-stalks, each of which branches after 8 inches into five small, tapering tentacles or tendrils, giving each stalk a total of 25 tentacles. […] Cannot yet assign positively to animal or vegetable kingdom, but odds now favour animal.[78]

A more perfect (and deliberate) account of the heterogeneous nature of the grotesque can be neither imagined nor improved upon[79]; "the grotesque consists in the very contrast that ominously permits of no reconciliation […] [which] totally destroys the order and deprives us of our foothold."[80] For Houellebecq, the style of scientific reporting adopted by Lovecraft "in his later stories operates according to the following principle: *the more monstrous and inconceivable the events and entities described, the more precise and clinical the description.* A scalpel is needed

78 Lovecraft, "At the Mountains of Madness," 19–21. Compare this passage with Kayser's historical account of the emergence of the grotesque: "By the word *grottesco* the Renaissance, which used it to designate a specific ornamental style suggested by antiquity, understood not only something playfully gay and carelessly fantastic, but also something ominous and sinister in the face of a world totally different from the familiar one—a world in which the realm of inanimate things is no longer separated from those of plants, animals, and human beings, and where the laws of statics, symmetry, and proportion are no longer valid." Kayser, *The Grotesque in Art and Literature*, 21. The pseudo-clinical revelation of the radical hybridity of the Old Ones is discursively tantamount to the suspension of transcendental reason in the unmediated encounter with the grotesque.
79 For Houellebecq, Lovecraft "is the first to have discovered the poetic impact of topology; to have shuddered in the face of Goedel's work on incomplete systems of formal logic. The vaguely repulsive implications of such strange axiomatic constructs were undoubtedly necessary for the dark entities of the Cthulhu cycle to emerge." Houellebecq, *H.P. Lovecraft*, 75. This reenforces Lovecraft's status as the maestro of fusion monstrosity.
80 Kayser, *The Grotesque in Art and Literature*, 59.

to dissect the un-nameable."[81] I agree, but I would go one step further. It is the novel materialism of Lovecraft's weird tale, the by-product of the artistic re-imagining of a virulent racism in accordance with the canons of the aesthetics of the grotesque, that allows him to successfully pull off his greatest literary trick: the hybridization of the grotesque with the sublime.[82] The unprecedented juxtaposition of the abject bodies of the Old Ones with the formalist epistemology of the medical examination discursively migrates the text from the merely grotesque to the (post-)Kantian sublime — the faculties of the *cogito* itself are parodied through their naïve deployment in the presence of the inconceivably and irreducibly heterogeneous object that is itself the signifier of an infinite time–space continuum.[83]

In the final analysis this heterogeneity is no less a political problem than it is a biological one: alterity renders the parapo-

---

[81] Houellebecq, *H.P. Lovecraft*, 79. Emphasis in the original. See also ibid., 74: "If there is a tone one does not expect to find in the horror story, it's that of a dissection report. [...] It would seem to be a discovery he made alone: that using science's vocabulary can serve as an extraordinary stimulant to the poetic imagination. The precise, minutely detailed content, dense and theoretical, encyclopedic in its perspective, produces a hallucinatory and thrilling effect." This accords perfectly with Harpham's definition of the grotesque: "In all of the examples that I have been considering, the sense of the grotesque arises with the perception that something is illegitimately in something else. The most mundane of figures, this metaphor of co-presence, *in*, also harbors the essence of the grotesque, the sense that things that should be kept apart are fused together." Harpham, *On the Grotesque*, 11.

[82] It should also be pointed out that this maneuver enables him to introduce an element of fascination, or *mysterium*, into his account of the uncanny Wholly Other. As Otto brilliantly expresses it, the "daemonic-divine object may appear to the mind as an object of horror and dread, but at the same time it is no less something that allures with a potent charm, and the creature, who trembles before it, utterly cowed and cast down, has always at the same time the impulse to turn to it, nay even to make it somehow his own." Otto, *The Idea of the Holy*, 31. By the end of this weird tale, the narrator has become hopelessly seduced by the artistic and scientific achievements of the Elder Ones.

[83] The "multiform descriptive methods of science [...] all serve to evoke a multi-faceted universe where the most heterogeneous fields of knowledge intersect and converge to generate the poetic trance that accompanies the revelation of forbidden truths." Houellebecq, *H.P. Lovecraft*, 76–77.

litical "nameless" inherently inassimilable into the onto-political discursive framework of liberalism, which is governed by an un-reconstituted representational theory of language. Lovecraft's racially spawned monsters (or Wholly Others), whose hybridity is the sign of miscegenation, double as the signifiers of the failure of orthodox liberalism: as the cross-bred hybrid, they are the unassimilable remnant within the ultra-neutralism of the bourgeois politics of modernity — the bearers of a radical, but indivisible, subjectivity, a sensible diversity that cannot be made subject to the requirements of the *ratio* of the public state.

> Singular analogies seem to be established between the foreigner and the monster, between the immigrant Kurd or Chinese and the "outsider." For Lovecraft [...] the displaying of these execrable mutants seems perhaps, in an obscure and confusing way, a testimonial to the failure of America's politics of racial assimilation, a deliberate rejection of the notion of the "melting pot," which forms so integral a part of the American dream.[84]

It is not unreasonable to view what is conventionally denoted conspiracy theory as the discursive "residue" of the crisis or state of emergency following the collective realization of the failure of liberal (neutralist) assimilation; the irreducible "diversity" of the Other yields the pluralistic exercise of an extra-judicial clandestine power, the phantasmagorical "Fifth Column."

> It is the Kurds, we note, those foreigners with repugnant faces, who by their impious cults have revived certain sleeping forces of evil. Clandestinely installed amid garbage and stench, in one of the many areas where no efficacious police control is possible, they support this secret horror, which, by slow internal corruption, insidiously undermines the foundation of the most prestigious city in the United States. Under the skyscrapers of New York, these subterranean avenues

---

84 Levy, *Lovecraft*, 61.

> branch out, opening on infamous cesspools, flowing into
> black and putrid rivers where primordial horrors swim.[85]

The unassimilable nature of the Monster/Wholly Other serves as the semiotic precondition for the emergence of the extra-judicial (non-rational, or "anti-Euclidean") parapolitical space of a race-based conspiratorial politics, grounded upon an irreducible moral and epistemological relativism: "They form, at the heart of American society, irreducible, unassimilable nuclei, which menace it from within."[86] Within the referential system of the Cthonoi, they are the black and mindless denizens of the anti-demi-god of liminal spaces and thresholds, YOG-SOTHOTH THE ALL-IN-ONE, THE ONE-IN-ALL (a.k.a., THE LURKER AT THE THRESHOLD; THE KEY TO THE GATE, WHEREBY THE SPHERES MEET[87]) who, along with the other ultra-nomadic power, Cthulhu (whose worshippers are malformed mulattoes), are the primary subjects of the master-text of clandestine reality, the *Necronomicon*: "The Inadmissable, which is also the Abominable [...]. The Impossible, which is the Evil, gnaws secretly at the very foundation of American civilization."[88] In short, the anti-gods of the Cthonoi are the criminal sovereigns of parapolitics: "criminals behaving as sovereigns and sovereigns behaving as criminals in a systematic ways."[89] The ultimate blasphemous truth is simply this: the Old Ones, the denizens of the parallel domains, are the true creators of the visible realms.

> [V]ertebrates, as well as an infinity of other life-forms — animal and vegetable, marine, terrestrial, and aerial — were the products of unguided evolution acting on life-cells made by the Old Ones but escaping beyond their radius of attention. They had been suffered to develop unchecked because they

---

85 Ibid., 66.
86 Ibid., 90.
87 Harms, *The Cthulhu Mythos Encyclopedia*, 327–28.
88 Levy, *Lovecraft*, 63.
89 Cribb, "Introduction: Parapolitics, Shadow Governance and Criminal Sovereignty," 1.

had not come in conflict with the dominant beings. Bothersome forms, of course, were mechanically exterminated. It interested us to see in some of the very last and most decadent sculptures a shambling primitive mammal, used sometimes for food and sometimes as an amusing buffoon by [the Old Ones], whose vaguely simian and human foreshadowings were unmistakable.[90]

Cosmic disinterestism with a grotesque vengeance.[91]

The lynchpin of the grotesque that underlies the meta-narrative conceit of the Mythos is that the (medically dissected) Elder Things of "At the Mountains of Madness" are identical with the (clairvoyantly announced) Old Ones cited in the *Necronomicon* of Abdul Al-Hazred. The shadowy presence of the "mad Arab" takes on an even greater significance that Lovecraft consciously allows when we see him within the terms not of literary cosmic horror but of parapolitical metaphor. In his mock account of "The History of the *Necronomicon*," Lovecraft provides us with the following: A "mad poet" originally from Sanaa in Yemen, c. 700 CE, who

spent ten years alone in the great southern desert of Arabia — the Roba el Khaliyeh or 'Empty Space' of the ancients — and 'Dahna' or 'Crimson' desert of the modern Arabs, which is held to be inhabited by protective evil spirits and monsters of death. [...] He was only an indifferent Moslem, worshipping unknown entities whom he called Yog-Sothoth and Cthulhu.[92]

---

90 Lovecraft, "At the Mountains of Madness," 63.
91 "Lovecraft never passes up an opportunity to diminish human accomplishments. [...] The guiding principle [of the Cthulhu Mythos is always] the same: the utter decimation [*sic*] of human self-importance by the attribution of a grotesque or contemptible origin of our species." Joshi, *H.P. Lovecraft: The Decline of the West*, 142 and 141. Lovecraft's paramount concern was with abjection.
92 Lovecraft, "The History of the *Necronomicon*," 311.

In other words: a deranged Arab visionary, in occult communion with invisible global forces, who has secretly wandered the shadowy domains of Arabia and Yemen, and then created a worldwide underground cult whose followers, penetrating the hidden byways and passages of the grotesque political bodies and spaces of diverse world-cities, have formed themselves into an underground anti-religion/death-cult committed to the overthrow of the West and the destruction of a civilization grounded upon pure reason through the performance of encrypted blasphemous rites.

This is almost too good to be true.

5. N. Lat. 40.7117°, W. Long. 74.0125°
08:46-09:03 AM, September 11, 2001

> The sky will burn at forty-five degrees altitude,
> Fire approaches the great new city,
> Immediately a huge, scattered flame leaps up,
> When they want to have verification from the Normans
> — Nostradamus, Century 6, Quatrain 97

> A priori principles are the conditions under which one
> conceives the ordered system of nature. The 'laws of nature' and
> all concepts of objects are specifications of the a priori forms:
> thus the 'objective reality' of phenomena consists in their
> conformity to the laws of the systems as constituted.
> — Ortega y Gasset

> The fantastic, after all, is perhaps nothing more than a
> heart-rendering revelation of the absurd, seeking to dislodge
> the reader from his normal states of mind and his familiar
> certitudes…
> — Maurice Levy

R'lyeh is the carnivalesque inversion of New York City: the highrising city that sinks turned inside-out is the sunken city that rises. Carnival is the "site" of both time and space, where the high and the low change places and temporarily enter into an absolute liminality; where the sublime and the grotesque are (orgiastically) celebrated as the complementary expressions of the primal heterogeneity of the nameless.[1]

It should come as no shock (brain-blasting or otherwise) to learn that the world-shattering collapse of two Cyclopean towers was subliminally prophesized in a seminal "Bush era" text on national security, *Rebuilding America's Defenses,* prepared by the Project for the New American Century (September 2000): "The process of transformation [of national defence policy], even if it brings revolutionary change, is likely to be a long one, absent some catastrophic and catalysing event — like a new Pearl Harbor."[2] The "shock and awe" of the spectacle of the collapsing Twin Towers, as we all know, so paralysed and overloaded our collective perceptions and understandings of events that we were "incapable of resistance" to the mutant-like expansion of the proliferating "War on Terror," which I have defined elsewhere as "a war of images and sounds, rather than objects and things," the manifestation of "the unprecedented limits imposed on subjective perception by the instrumental splitting of modes of perception and representation," attaining its apotheosis in "the will to universalised illumination."[3] In other words, living through "the War on Terror," just like the antecedent "Gulf War," is very much like watching television, or cinema. (A personal anecdote might be in order here. In February 2010 I was in New York City for the first time since 9/11. Naturally, I asked as many New Yorkers as possible about their experiences on September 11. Literally all of them who witnessed the Twin Towers attack in person recalled that the event was like "watching a movie.") It comes as no surprise, then, that "the War on Terror," consisting of the fast-moving (24/7) manipulation of sensory bombardment (the "news cycle"), should be so dependent upon psychological disorientation for success; the public state is now revealed as the "space" of deep politics, full-spectrum dominance and "shock and awe" inaugurating a catastrophic collapse of the allegedly

---

1 See Bakhtin, *Rabelais and His World.*
2 Scott, *The Road to 9/11,* 193.
3 See Wilson, "Crimes against Reality."

fixed boundaries between external and internal space(s) that yields a new "post-liberal" unitary space of war and media representation. 9/11 collectively brutalizes us through chaos and simulation; because we are brutalized we are traumatized. Because we suffer from collective trauma, we experience "reality" in an irrational dream-like state, in which the reality principle, the ontological and epistemological foundation of liberal and democratic discourse, is suspended. It is through the suspension of the reality principle that the Dual State is ultimately able to exist.

As a result, the contemporary scholar of parapolitics, such as Scott, exists in a state of mourning — and abject denial. Scott mourns the death of the public, democratic, and liberal state. His resultant denial is a symptom of the trauma inflicted upon his phenomenological self through the parapolitical irruption signified by the "American War Machine." Scott is the trauma "victim" of the parapolitical disappearance of the American democratic public state into the dualistic post-9/11 Deep State. And even if Scott's prose does not display evidence of trauma, his poetry — an even more reliable guide to the "real" of the unconscious — clearly does.[4] Employing poetics rather than prose, Scott conveys with inimical style the essence of our parapolitical being, "split-mindedness."

> is not my inability / to change all this / but my speaking with two voices / which cannot be compassed / having to be split-minded / in the struggle to keep communication / between the present / and the best of the past / there is not much progress / if the left leg hankers for the beach / and the right for Sacramento / the problem has always been / how do we live with evil / we can profit from it / we can preach against it /

[4] Scott is generally considered America's foremost author of political poetry. His works include *Coming to Jakarta: A Poem About Terror*, *Listening to the Candle: A Poem on Impulse*, *Minding the Darkness: A Poem for the Year 2000*, and *Mosaic Orpheus*.

> but if we write poetry / how not to misrepresent / the great conspiracy / of organized denial / we call civilization?[5]

As Scott compellingly demonstrates, split-mindedness is the master-sign of the Dual State: the un-humanist faculties of perception necessary for the operation of the parapolitical have been inscribed directly into our phenomenological body-self through trauma. Anticipating the dual charge of either sensationalism or paranoia, Scott claims that he speaks "as one who believes passionately in civilization, and fears that by excessive denial our own civilization may indeed be becoming threatened."[6]

In other words, he sounds like Francis Wayland Thurston.

Just as with Scott's poetics, "Lovecraft's literature gives precise and alarming meaning to the celebrated dictum, 'a deliberate disordering of the senses.'"[7] The critical difference between them is that the master-signs of the "terrestrial" horror of the Dual State are not the (garbage) inter-dimensional cosmic antigods of the Chthonoi, but the all-too-human psychotic/idiot archons of the New World Order[8]: CIA, NSA, NRO, NGIP, GDIP, SIGINT,[9] and PRISM.[10] And with Edward Snowden as the new "Randolph Carter."[11]

---

5   Scott, *Minding the Darkness*, 137.
6   Scott, *Deep Politics and the CIA Global Drug Connection*, 2–3.
7   Houellebecq, *H.P. Lovecraft*, 69.
8   See Engdahl, *Full Spectrum Dominance*. For a compelling account of the "demiurgic" elements governing the "occult" manipulation of the transition from British to American hegemony within the world-system and the parallel convergence of the anglocentric national intelligence complexes, see the same author's *A Century of War* and *The Gods of Money*.
9   The Central Intelligence Agency; The National Security Agency, a.k.a. "The Puzzle Factory"; The National Reconnaissance Office; The National Geo-Spatial Intelligence Program; The General Defense Intelligence Program and Signals Intelligence, respectively.
10 The monstrosity recently revealed by Edward Snowden; in the Lovecraftian frame of reference, yet one more incarnation of AZATHOTH, the blind idiot anti-god who mindlessly babbles and blasphemes at the center of Ultimate Chaos. Harms, *The Cthulhu Mythos Encyclopedia*, 14–15.
11 Lovecraft's eponymous "stand-in" and the (anti-)hero of five of his most Dunsany-esque tales: "The Dream-Quest of Unknown Kadath" (1927), "The

The conspiracy narrative is the weird tale of parapolitics. Therefore, any literary theory of the parapolitical would have to be premised upon the twin columns of the post-Kantian sublime and the classical aesthetic of the grotesque. I argue that Lovecraft's greatest artistic accomplishment, one that is almost wholly unrecognized in voluminous annals of "Lovecraft Studies," is his successful synthesis of the grotesque with the sublime through his radically anti-Kantian approach to space–time; as the signifiers of an annihilating infinity, the ontological ground of all objects of perception is rendered tantamount to a grotesquerie, within and through which the chaotically heterogeneous prevails: within infinity, nothing can be precluded.[12] The aesthetic "problem" that Lovecraft presents the contemporary critic is that of the high artist of the low form; as modern literature is premised upon humanism, it has proven difficult to situate within the canon an un-humanist writer of the weird tale whose signature notion of character development is the transcendental-negating shriek of the annihilation of the self. The cosmic horror of Lovecraft is itself the site of the (counter-intuitive) unification of the sublime with the grotesque[13] through its singular elevation to high literature of that most ignoble of objects: racism. Racism and racial paranoia is the true meta-narrative thread of the later works, providing the thematic and stylistic unity of the seminal Mythos; the weird tales of Cthulhu are, in fact, extensive re-writings of the earlier tales composed under the rubric of a twin set of antinomies: sublime/conspiracy and grotesque/race. Racism is the template of the Lovecraftian proj-

Silver Key" (1926), "Through the Gates of the Silver Key" (1933), "The Case of Charles Dexter Ward" (1927), and, most famously, "The Statement of Randolph Carter" (1919).

12 "Lovecraft's body of work can be compared to a gigantic dream machine, of astounding breadth and efficacy. […] Today, it stands before us, an imposing baroque structure, its towering strata rising in so many layered concentric circles, a wide and sumptuous landing around each — the whole surrounding a vortex of pure horror and absolute marvel." Houellebecq, *H.P. Lovecraft*, 42 and 40.

13 Throughout his work Kayser employs the "abysmal" as a synonym for the grotesque.

ect — it is also what forces him to migrate into the domain of the parapolitical. Employed as a literary device, racism can only give rise to one narrative device: reverse colonization. I am very much in agreement with David E. Schultz's view that the canonical texts of the Cthulhu Mythos are, in essence, re-writings of the earlier weird tales but now repositioned along the lines of racist conspiracy narrative.[14] The "high" literary work of racism, therefore, must necessarily invoke the stylistic techniques of the conspiracy narrative which, in turn, requires an engagement with the covert.

Although the greater part of this essay has discussed Lovecraft's aesthetics in terms of the Kantian, it would be useful for what follows to make a (mercifully) brief detour through the Hegelian. The relevance of Hegel to the weird tale is clear from a cursory reading of the philosopher's notorious commentary[15] on the "fantastic symbolism" of Indian art, an objectively inferior form of symbolic art, the most primitive form of aesthetic production that stands "as the threshold of art" but which "belongs especially to the East."[16] What Hegel finds most objectionable in Indian art is its infinite repetition (re. Burke) of gigantic grotesque statues,[17] which, in the Hegelian view, violates the essential aesthetic principle the adequate expression "of the Idea of the beautiful as the Ideal of art."[18] The true sublime in art always assumes the form of a "finite appearance" that "expresses the Absolute, which it is supposed to bring before our vision, but only in such a way that the Absolute withdraws from the appearance and the appearance falls short of the content."[19] To do otherwise is to commit the fatal artistic mistake of confounding the particular with the universal, which, as the sign of the Absolute,[20] is,

---

14 See Schultz, "From Microcosm to Macrocosm."
15 Hegel, *Aesthetics*, 332–37.
16 Ibid., 303.
17 Kayser, *The Grotesque in Art and Literature*, 100–103.
18 Hegel, *Aesthetics*, 299.
19 Ibid., 339.
20 "'Absolute,' 'absolute Idea,' 'absolute meaning,' 'absolute Concept,' all appear [in Hegel's writings] [...] as synonyms for God." Knox, "Translator's Pref-

at any given moment in history, inexhaustible (infinite) and incapable of limited, or exhaustive, representation; therefore, the aesthetic deformity of Indian art — as with all forms of "fantastic symbolism"[21] — is precisely that the imagination "can have no recourse but to distortions, since it drives particular shapes beyond their firmly limited particular character, stretches them, alters them into indefiniteness, and intensifies them beyond all bounds."[22] Critical here is Hegel's profoundly metaphysical view of art: historically, artistic production is the mind's first attempt, via imagination and the sensuous, to realize the universal: "It is with this attempt [...] [to heal the breach within] the immediately intuited identity between the Absolute and its externally perceived existence [...] that there arises the proper need for art."[23] Just as the "innermost and essential nature" of mind is thought,[24] so too the essential nature of man is to realize the

---

ace," xiv. See below.

21 Hegel, *Aesthetics,* 332–47.
22 Ibid., 334. Broadly put: the fantastic symbolist has committed a category error among the universal, the particular, and the individual.
23 Ibid., 332-33. The most clear and concise explanation of this notion of the "breach" within reality that demands the coming forth of art is offered by T.M. Knox, and I will repeat it here. "The complete correspondence between concept and reality is not to be found anywhere in nature, or even in human beings in so far as they are bodies or sensuous beings. This is because things external to one another cannot completely correspond with concepts or categories which, as thoughts, form a whole internally interconnected. It is when man's mind has risen to self-consciousness as spirit that in spirit and its productions the oppositions between universal and particular, subject and object, ideal and real, divine and human, are ultimately *reconciled* in a concrete unity. Knowledge and fact may, at the intellectual level of natural science, be opposed to one another as universal to particular, but, when, the fact known is man's spiritual self, knower and known become a unity in which the difference between the two is not expunged but retained and *mediated* or reconciled. [...] The background of all of this is theological." Knox, "Translator's Preface," ix–x. Emphases in the original.
24 "Thought — to think — is precisely that in which the mind has its innermost and essential nature. In gaining this [symbolic] thinking consciousness concerning itself and its products, the mind is behaving according to its essential nature, however much freedom and caprice those products may display." Hegel, *Introductory Lectures,* 14–15.

"Absolute"[25] through the promulgation of universal categories of (self-) consciousness — the "concept."[26] Hence, "The universal need for expression in art lies, therefore, in man's rational impulse to exalt the inner and outer world into a spiritual consciousness for himself, as an object in which he recognizes his own self."[27] It should come as no surprise, then, that any form of art that is the medium of expression for an infinite proliferation of hybridity should fail the Hegelian litmus test for spiritual consciousness.

> In order, as sensuous figures themselves, to reach universality, the individual figures are wildly tugged apart from one another into the colossal and the grotesque. For the individual figure which is to express not itself and the meaning appropriate to it as a particular phenomenon but a universal meaning lying outside its own, does not satisfy contemplation until it is torn out of itself into monstrosity without aim or measure. For here above all there is the most extravagant exaggeration of size, alike in the spatial figure and in temporal incommensurability, as well as the multiplication of one and the same characteristic, the many heads, the mass of arms, etc., whereby the attainment of the breadth and universality of meanings is pursued.[28]

---

25 Hegel's weakly disguised version of God always assumes the *particular* form of the Lutheran. "For not only is there divinity in man, but in him its operative under a form that is appropriate to the essence of God, in a mode quite other and higher in nature. God is a Spirit [*Geist*; the Absolute], and it is only in man that the medium through which the divine element passes has the form of conscious spirit, that actively realizes itself." Ibid., 34.
26 "For thinking requires self-consciousness which sets an object before itself in order to find itself therein." Hegel, *Aesthetics*, 335.
27 Hegel, *Introductory Lectures*, 36.
28 Hegel, *Aesthetics*, 338. The spirit of this remarkable passage is captured perfectly in one of the early Mythos tales, "The Case of Charles Dexter Ward": "It is hard to explain just how a single sight of a tangible object with measurable dimensions could so shake and change a man; and we may only say that there is about certain outlines and entities a power of symbolism and suggestion which acts frightfully on a sensitive thinker's perspective and whispers terrible hints of obscure cosmic relationships and un-nameable

Therefore, Indian art is not beautiful.

> True beauty [...] we may not seek in this field of murky confusion. [...] [Aesthetic] imagination [...] tears [shapes] apart from one another and therefore in this struggle towards accord brings to light only the very opposite in its lack of reconciliation. [...] [The Indian's] chief defect, compatibility with the general nature of this stage [of art], consists in this, that they cannot grasp either the meanings themselves in their clarity, or existing reality in its own proper shape and significance.[29]

Nor is Indian art understood as sublime "properly so-called"[30]; it is the "flight beyond the determinateness of appearance [that] constitutes the general character of the sublime."[31] Whereas "in the true sublime, a sharp consciousness of inadequacy is required,"[32] since the Hegelian sublime is nothing other than the proposition that "God is the creator of the universe. This is the purest expression of the sublime itself,"[33] the investiture of the particular with the concept "is at variance with the Indian pressure to refer each and everything back to the sheerly Absolute and Divine, and to contemplate in the commonest and most sensuous things a fancifully created presence and actuality of the gods."[34] What Hegel does grant the fantastic symbolism

---

realities behind the protective illusions of common vision." Lovecraft, "The Case of Charles Dexter Ward," 181.
29 Hegel, *Aesthetics*, 334.
30 Ibid., 340.
31 Ibid., 303.
32 Hegel, cited in Clayborough, *The Grotesque in English Literature*, 31.
33 Hegel, *Aesthetics*, 373. More precisely: "In sublimity [...] external existence, in which the substance [of the object] is brought before contemplation is degraded in comparison with the substance, since this degradation and servitude is the one and only way whereby the one can be illustrated in art; this is because the *one* God is explicitly without shape and is incapable of expression in his *positive* essence in anything finite and mundane." Ibid., 372. Emphases in the original.
34 Ibid., 334-35.

of India, however, is an inferior form of the sublime: *sublime pantheism*,[35] an almost Burkean phenomenon in which the imperfect conceptualization of the Absolute resides "as immanent in the specific appearances as the soul that produces and animates them, and now in this immanence is viewed as *affirmatively* present, and is grasped and presented by the individual who is self-abandoning owing to his ecstatic immersion in this essence that dwells in all these things."[36]

What is vital in these passages is the manner in which Hegel achieves (probably by accident) a pseudo-synthesis of the sublime and the grotesque: the chaotic amalgamations of dissimilar forms multiplied to the level of magnitude within Indian religious art evidence the lack, or absence, of true spiritual consciousness which would be the (otherwise) correct expression of the universalized concept of the Absolute. The ultimate limitation, or failure, of fantastic symbolism lies within its inability to overcome its own naivety and appreciate the objective inadequacy of the grotesque form to truthfully express the concept of the universal. However, in every particular instance, "the grotesque implies a transcendence of the individual form toward a realm inhabited by supernatural powers" — or monsters.[37] What is most remarkable in all of this should by now be clear: in his very final works Lovecraft defies Hegel and succeeds in turning fantastic symbolism into great literary art. And he accomplishes this tour de force by summoning the spirit (*Geist*) of the greatest anti-Hegelian philosopher of them all and whose thought, as I hope to show, stands behind all that is most aesthetically worthwhile within Lovecraft's oeuvre.

No other weird tale of Lovecraft demonstrates with greater perfection the unavoidable collision between cosmic horror, race conspiracy, and clandestine para-reality than his late masterpiece "The Shadow over Innsmouth" (1931). Yet one more tale of reverse colonization set on the level of cosmic horror, the text

---

35 Ibid., 364–71. In essence, "mysticism."
36 Ibid., 320–21.
37 Kayser, *The Grotesque in Art and Literature*, 102.

is concerned with an inter-generational conspiracy of miscegenation and anti-human cross-breeding between the degenerate inhabitants of an ancient (and secret passageway-riddled) New England fishing town and the amphibiously humanoid "The Deep Ones," who are the denizens of the submarine anti-demigod DAGON, the archdeacon of the heresiarch Cthulhu. The conspiracy narrative of reverse colonization is made as plain as it is simple.

> The Deep Ones could never be destroyed, even though the palaeogean magic of the forgotten Old Ones might sometimes check them. For the present they would rest; but some day, if they remembered, they would rise again for the tribute Great Cthulhu craved. It would be a city greater than Innsmouth next time. They had planned to spread, and had brought up that which would help them, but now they must wait once more.[38]

As we can now predict, the outline of the conspiracy against the (un-)human race is made out through the alterity of the two central aesthetic pillars of fantastic symbolism, the grotesque and the sublime. First, the grotesque.

> And yet I saw them in a limitless stream — flopping, hopping, croaking, bleating — surging inhumanly through the spectral moonlight in a grotesque, malignant saraband of fantastic nightmare […] and one, who led the way, was clad in a ghoulishly humped black coat and striped trousers, and had a man's felt hat perched on the shapeless thing that answered for a head. […] Their croaking, baying voices, clearly used for articulate speech, held all the dark shades of expression which their staring faces lacked.[39]

Then, the sublime.

---

38 Lovecraft, "The Shadow over Innsmouth," 391.
39 Ibid., 385.

> I shall plan my cousin's[40] escape from [...] [the] madhouse, and together we shall go to marvel-shrouded Innsmouth. We shall swim out to that brooding reef in the sea and dive down through black abysses to Cyclopean and many-columned Y'ha-nthlei, and in that lair of the Deep Ones we shall dwell amidst wonder and glory forever.[41]

But now something unexpected happens; the uninterrupted movement between the parallel domains of the sublime and the grotesque are textually "disrupted" by the irruption of the clandestine agencies of the State.

> During the winter of 1927–28 officials of the Federal government made a strange and secret investigation of certain conditions in the ancient Massachusetts seaport of Innsmouth. The public first learned of it in February, when a vast series of raids and arrests occurred, followed by the deliberate burning and dynamiting—under suitable precautions—of an enormous number of crumbling, worm-eaten, and supposedly empty houses along the abandoned waterfront. Uninquiring souls let this occurrence pass as one of the major clashes in a spasmodic war on liquor.[42]

Unexpected because nowhere else does Lovecraft so explicitly evoke the national security apparatus of the government, thus establishing with the single stroke of a pen the central hypothesis of UFO conspiracy theory: the occluded existence of a clandestine governmental department devoted to both investigating and suppressing reports of extraterrestrial activity; not power/

---

40 This is Lawrence Marsh, who has been incarcerated in a sanitarium in Canton, Ohio, because of an incurable case of atavistic regression. The narrator highlights the fact that "poor little cousin Lawrence" was an "almost perfect duplicate of his grandmother" who had been born in the daemonically infested accursed community of Arkham and who had disappeared following the suicide of her only son, the narrator's uncle Douglas. Ibid., 388.
41 Ibid., 392.
42 Ibid., 329.

knowledge but power/containment. It is an underappreciated aspect of Lovecraft's literary style that he restricts his cosmic apocalypses wholly to the private sphere, judiciously avoiding any situation that would logically compel statist intervention.[43] Yet, under a more nuanced reading, not unexpected at all; given the parapolitical nature of the Lovecraftian landscape, defensive action in covert form is precisely what we should expect. This un-knowledge has, in fact, been hiding in plain sight throughout the entirety of Lovecraft's oeuvre.

> Keener news-followers, however, wondered at the prodigious number of arrests, the abnormally large force of men used in making them, and the secrecy surrounding the disposal of the prisoners. No trials, or even definite charges, were reported; nor were any of the captives seen thereafter in the regular gaols of the nation. There were vague statements about disease and concentration camps, and later about dispersal in various naval and military prisons, but nothing positive ever developed. Innsmouth itself was left almost depopulated, and is even now only beginning to shew signs of a sluggishly revived existence.[44]

Incredibly, what we are witnessing is Homeland Security in full operation exactly seventy years early.

> Complaints from many liberal organizations were met with long confidential discussions, and representatives were taken on trips to certain camps and prisons. As a result, these societies became surprisingly passive and reticent. Newspaper men were harder to manage, but seemed largely to cooperate with the government in the end. Only one paper — a tabloid always discounted because of its wild policy — mentioned the deep-diving submarine that discharged torpedoes down-

---

43 To the best of my knowledge, Harman is the only commentator to have picked up on this. Harman, *Weird Realism*, 175–77.
44 Lovecraft, "The Shadow over Innsmouth," 329.

> ward in the marine abyss just beyond Devil Reef. That item, gathered by chance in a haunt of sailors, seemed indeed rather far-fetched, since the low, black reef lies a full mile and a half out from Innsmouth Harbor.[45]

As far as I can tell, the invocation of a material self-defense mobilized in response to the crypto-occultist invasion is expressly referenced in only two other tales: the somewhat inconsequential police raid in "The Horror at Red Hook" and the narrator's desperate plea to the Academy of Sciences at the end of "The Mountains of Madness." I would go so far as to suggest a hidden parapolitical story arc linking "At the Mountains of Madness" with "The Shadow over Innsmouth." In the former, the narrator declares that his only reason for saying the un-sayable ("I have been forced into speech because men of science have refused to follow my advice without knowing why"[46]) is in order to preempt the departure of the Starkweather–Moore expedition to Antarctica — which now stands revealed as the infernal "Plains of Leng" darkly hinted at in the *Necronomicon*[47] (in truth, the distinct possibility is raised in the reader's mind that the follow-up expedition is really a cover for a clandestine investigation). All three weird tales beautifully recycle a stock device of the conspiracy narrative, "the cover-up." And, if all of this is not enough, comes the piece-de-resistance, the ultimate cliché of the conspiracy narrative — the "true" confession of the whistleblower, the anonymous purveyor of inside knowledge: "But at last I am going to defy the ban on speech about this thing."[48]

But with one singular difference.

This narrator does *not* scream.

Or, more precisely, he only screams *once*, when he undergoes an oneiric vision of the abased genetically crafted slaves of the Ancient Ones: "This was the dream in which I saw a *shog-*

---

45 Ibid., 329–30.
46 Lovecraft, "At the Mountains of Madness," 1.
47 Harman, *Weird Realism*, 169–70.
48 Lovecraft, "The Shadow over Innsmouth," 330.

goth[49] for the first time, and the sight set me awake in a frenzy of screaming. That morning the mirror definitely told me I had acquired *the Innsmouth look*."[50] For the illiterate among us, the "Innsmouth look" is local dialect for the assembly of genetic markers of the in-bred residents of Innsmouth resulting from their bestial/cross-species miscegenation with the monstrously amphibious Deep Ones, known folkloricistically throughout the rustic and back-water zones of north-eastern Massachusetts; "Clearly, in the eyes of the educated, Innsmouth was merely an exaggerated case of civic degeneration."[51] The cosmic joke that Lovecraft sadistically plays on his as always hapless protagonist is the one that the reader has been silently aware of for quite some time: that the narrator is a direct descendant of the patriarch of Innsmouth, Obed Marsh, the sea-faring ancestor who originally forged the interracial link with the Deep Ones in the mid-19th century.[52] The Wholly Other is revealed as the secret sharer of the self.

But he does not scream.

What is truly remarkable here is that the narrator's realization of his biological affiliation with the mutants of Innsmouth does not culminate in a brain-blasting, but, rather, an almost

---

49 One of Lovecraft's singular and signature creations that is almost impossible to define. Ben Woodard has mischievously identified the Shoggoth with the more generic "muck monster," the embodiment of fungal life. Essentially a sentient form of protoplasm bio-genetically engineered by the Old Ones, the defining trait of the Shoggoth is their undulating, protoplasmic formlessness. The reduction of a gigantic life form to the wholly fungal constitutes the epitome of the Lovecraftian abject, depriving the humanistic solidity of the body of its "fixed boundaries, complicating the differences between sense and thought, between life as bound and life as creeping. Philosophically speaking, muck monsters provide a degradation of phenomenology in that thought becomes another object in the pile of nature and [is] not the sole means of determining nature through the senses" — the governing conceit of Cartesian modernity. Woodward, *Slime Dynamics*, 38. Fungi is abject precisely because it is the biological embodiment of a literally form-less life; the poetics of slime, from Yuggoth or elsewhere, *is* abjection.

50 Lovecraft, "The Shadow over Innsmouth," 333.

51 Ibid., 335.

52 Ibid., 331–35 and 386–90.

erotic surrender to the Wholly Other, which, according to Otto, is the benign aspect of *stupor*.

> In the winter of 1930–1 [...] the dreams began. They were very sparse and insidious at first, but increased in frequency and vividness as the weeks went by. Great watery spaces opened before me, and I seemed to wander through titanic sunken porticos and labyrinths of weedy Cyclopean walls with grotesque fishes as my companions. Then the *other shapes* began to appear, filling me with nameless horror the moment I awoke. But during the dreams they did not horrify me at all — I was one with them, wearing their unhuman trappings, treading their aqueous ways, and praying monstrously at their evil sea-bottom temples.[53]

If Edmund Burke had been commissioned to design a submarine city he could scarcely have done better. Against all odds, Lovecraft has finally decided to write about (a kind of) love. If I were to generalize greatly, "The Shadow over Innsmouth" possibly marks a return, by means of thematic inversion, to the more beguiling fantasies, or wonderment, of his earlier pre-Mythos works which were written very much under the influence of Lord Dunsany — sublimely terrifying, to be sure, but largely free of the abject. Which is to say, most of these Dunsany-esque weird fantasies were all written before Lovecraft's sojourn in Brooklyn.[54]

---

53 Ibid., 390.
54 In Lovecraft's "The Doom That Came to Sarnath" (1920), there is a very faint but clear anticipation of the anthropoid fish-frog denizens of Innsmouth: "It is written on the brick cylinders of Kadatheron that the beings of Ib were in hue as green as the lake and the mists that rise above it; and that they had bulging eyes, pouting, flabby lips, and curious ears, and were without voice. [...] [I]t is certain that they worshipped a sea-green stone idol chiseled in the likeness of Bokrug, the great water-lizard; before which they danced horribly when the moon was gibbous." Lovecraft, "The Doom That Came to Sarnath," 31. This is wholly consistent with the sense touched upon by Schultz and others that all of the Mythos tales are disguised re-workings of the pre-New York texts.

One night I had a frightful dream in which I met my grandmother under the sea. She lived in a phosphorescent palace of many terraces, with gardens of strange leprous corals and grotesque brachiate efflorescences, and welcomed me with a warmth that may have been sardonic.[55] She had changed — as those who take to the water change — and told me that she had never died. Instead, she had gone to a spot her dead son had learned about, and had leaped to a realm whose wonders — destined for him as well — he had spurned with a smoking pistol. This was to be my realm, too — I could not escape it. I would never die, but would live with those who had lived since before man ever walked the earth.[56]

Commenting upon this passage, Patricia MacCormack suggests that Lovecraft's later writings announce a partial reconciliation with liminality and the grotesque; for Lovecraft, "monsters are not aberrant versions of the Human. They are monstrous, that is, not in form, but on the levels of perception and possibility. What emerges in Lovecraft is that the human is a vague, strategic myth for ensuring sanity and thus traditional subjectivity through a belief in like relations."[57] Ironically, the radically anti-taxonomic but signature hybridity of the Lovecraftian Wholly Other compels the sensitive reader to adopt a far more nuanced response towards them/it precisely because the Monster–God's lack of homogeneity suggests the possibility of multiple interpretations: "The animal elements of the Ancient Ones, while residually named as animal, are in fact cephalopodan, insect and other adamantly non-mammalian forms."[58] And it is the manifesting presence of the Innsmouth look within the narrator him-

---

55 As Lovecraft somewhat chillingly puts it, "For bringing the upper-earth men's death I must do penance, but that would not be heavy." "The Shadow over Innsmouth," 391. As the narrator is an informant, one suspects that his shamanistic/numinous "dream quest" to the Deep Ones is actually a "lure."
56 Ibid., 391.
57 MacCormack, *Lovecraft through Deleuzio-Guattarian Gates*, 1.
58 Ibid., 4.

self that marks the preliminary linkage between the grotesque and the parallel eroticization of the monstrous body:

> So far I have not shot myself as my uncle Douglas did. I bought an automatic and almost took the step, but certain dreams deterred me. The tense extremes of horror are lessening, and I feel queerly drawn toward the unknown sea-deeps instead of fearing them. I hear and do strange things in sleep, and awake with a kind of exaltation instead of terror. I do not believe I need to wait for the full changes as most have waited. If I did, my father would probably shut me up in a sanitorium as my poor little cousin is shut up. Stupendous and unheard-of splendors await me below, and I shall seek them soon. *Ia-R'leh! Cthulhu fhtagn! Ia! Ia!* No, I shall not shoot myself — I cannot be made to shoot myself![59]

The narrator does not scream because he has successfully migrated from the sublime to the (properly) beautiful; to no longer scream, either in horror or in pain, is the essential function of Art. In no other tale more than "The Shadow over Innsmouth" does Lovecraft demonstrate his affiliation with Schopenhauer. In sharp distinction to Kant, a movement towards, or even a synthesis of the sublime and the beautiful is possible, based upon Schopenhauer's ontology of Will-as-Being. As with Kant, the sublime is understood in terms of the trans-human: "This is the full impression of the sublime. It is occasioned [...] by the sight of a power threatening the individual with annihilation, incomparably superior to him."[60] However, given that the purpose of aesthetic contemplation is to culminate in the suspension, rather than the excitation, of the Will, the perception of the sublime/super-human object may be deployed as a form of psychic narcotic.

---

59 Lovecraft, "The Shadows over Innsmouth," 391–92.
60 Schopenhauer, *The World as Will and Representation*, 250.

When we lose ourselves in contemplation of the infinite magnitude of the world in space and time, reflect on the millennia that have flowed past and on those to come — or indeed, when the night sky actually brings countless worlds before our eyes, and thus impresses the immensity of the world upon our consciousness — we feel ourselves reduced to nothingness, feel ourselves as individual, as animate body, as transitory phenomenon of will, vanishing like a drop in the ocean, dissipating into nothingness. But at the same time there rises against such a specter of our own nullity, against such a lying impossibility, the immediate consciousness that indeed all these worlds exist only in a presentation to us, only as modifications of the eternal subject of pure cognition that we find ourselves to be as soon as we forget individuality, and that is the necessary, the conditioning bearer of all worlds and of all times. The magnitude of the world that previously caused us unrest now rests within us; our dependence upon it is nullified by its dependence upon us. All of this does not enter reflection all at once, however, but shows itself as a merely felt consciousness that we are in some sense (which philosophy alone explicates) one with the world and thus not crushed, but lifted by its immensity. It is the felt consciousness of that which the Upanishads of the Vedas repeatedly pronounce in such manifold variations. [...] "All these creatures together am I, and beyond me no being exists" [...]. It is elevation above the particular individual that one is, the feeling of the sublime.[61]

Hence the decidedly anti-Kantian (and even more anti-Hegelian) title of Book Three, Chapter 41 of *The World as Will and Presentation*: "Everything Beautiful in its Own Way."[62] For the rapidly mutating narrator, the Deep Ones are no longer sublime but beautiful, this the perfect Lovecraftian expression of Schopenhauer's notion of the post-Kantian beautiful: "the object of

61 Ibid., 251.
62 Ibid., 254–58.

aesthetic contemplation is not the individual thing but the Idea [eternal Form] striving for revelation in it, i.e., an adequate objectivization of will on a particular level."[63] Schopenhauer's dynamic and immanent neo-Platonism allows him to overcome the dualistic Kantian divide between the sublime and the beautiful: the other *is* the self, which permits a de-centering iteration between *Homo sapiens* and *monstrum*.

> In calling an object *beautiful,* we thereby express the fact that it is an object of our aesthetic contemplation, which includes two things, namely, on the one hand, that our view of it makes us *objective,* i.e., that in the contemplation of it we are no longer conscious of ourselves as individuals, but as pure will-less subject of cognition, and on the other hand, that in the object we are taking cognizance not of the individual thing, but of an Idea, which can only happen so far as our contemplation of the object is not given over to [...] something beyond it [...] but rests upon the object itself.[64]

For Hegel this is pure anathema—which is precisely Schopenhauer's point. For the pseudo-theologian from Jena, there can be few thoughts more heretical than "Everything Beautiful in its Own Way."

> [T]he specific shape which every content of the Idea gives to itself in the particular forms of art is always adequate to that content, and the deficiency or consummation [like in India] lies only in the relatively untrue or true determinateness in which and as which the Idea is explicit to itself. This is be-

---

63 Ibid., 255.
64 Ibid. Emphases in the original. Note the translator's comment provided by Richard E. Aquila and David Carus on this otherwise unfathomable passage: "apart from the relevant sort of withdrawal or nullification of the will, we are not simply aware *of* objects as 'related' to our willing, but those objects themselves *reflect* that relation, i.e., in some way 'refer' to the very will in which they are related." Ibid.

cause the content must be true and concrete in itself before it can find its truly beautiful shape.[65]

But if there is any merit to this view at all, it can only be in relation to the human production of *fine art,* not natural beauty — which Hegel precludes in advance from constituting a valid subject of aesthetics, which "does not treat of beauty in general, but merely of *artistic* beauty."[66] Why this apparently arbitrary demarcation between nature and culture? As always with Hegel, it comes down to a question of *Geist*.

> We may [...] begin at once by asserting that artistic beauty stands *higher* than nature. For the beauty of art is the beauty that is born — born again, that is — of the mind [*Geist*]; and by as much as the mind and its products are higher than nature and its appearances, by so much the beauty of art is higher than the beauty of nature. Indeed, if we look at it *formally* — i.e., only considering in what way it exists, not what there is in it — even a silly fancy such as may pass through a man's head is higher than any product of nature; for such a fancy must at least be characterized by intellectual being and by freedom.[67]

But here idealism is revealed as nothing more than anthropocentrism with a Berlin pedigree — the very thing that Schopenhauer most puts into doubt through his unconditionally anti-humanist metaphysics of the will is the very possibility of segregating the human from the natural which underpins the entirety of Hegel's characteristically top-heavy system (or "science"). Schopenhauer's almost phenomenological migration from the sublime to the beautiful is nothing other than this very aesthetic contemplation whose objectivity is the unconscious, or intuitive, recognition of "the Thing" as an individualized ex-

---

65 Hegel, *Aesthetics*, 300.
66 Hegel, *Introductory Lectures*, 3.
67 Ibid., 4.

pression, within time and space, of the idea of that particular species. "I call the degree of objectification of will in a thing, that thing's substantial form.⁶⁸ [...] Every quality of matter is always also a phenomenon of an Idea and as such susceptible to the aesthetic regard, i.e., to cognizance of the Idea displayed in it"⁶⁹: in other words, the *entirety of all phenomena interpreted as aesthetic concepts.* It is surely not coincidental that in "The Shadow over Innsmouth," and no less in "At the Mountains of Madness," the seduction of the narrator's gaze is occasioned by the apperception of an entire alien species. Cthulhu remains wholly unclassifiable (*sui generis*); the Elder Ones and the Deep Ones do constitute their own class, which constitute the fleshy instantiation of one Idea-within-the-Will.

> Each thing has [...] its own peculiar beauty: not only everything organic and displayed within the unity of an individuality, but also every inorganic thing, formless things, even every artifact. For all of these reveal the Ideas through which will is objectified on the lowest levels, provide, as it were, the deepest, resonating bass tones of nature [...]. One thing is more beautiful than another, however, by the fact that it facilitates that purely objective regard, accommodates to it, even as it were compels one to it, in which case we then call it most beautiful. This sometimes occurs by the fact that, as an individual thing with the most distinct, purely determined, altogether significant relationship among its parts, it gives pure expression to the Idea of its species and, completely unifying within itself all possible expression of its species, completely reveals the latter's Idea, thus considerably facilitating the observer's passage from the individual thing to the Idea and just by that fact also the state of pure contemplativeness.⁷⁰

---

68 Schopenhauer, *The World as Will and Representation*, 267.
69 Ibid., 260.
70 Ibid., 256. Discussing the debate over eugenics and immigration in early 20th century America, Lovett-Graff has offered a materialist/biological version of the metaphysical/aesthetic argument that I am providing: "Lovecraft cannily capitalizes on the analogies post-Darwinian [*sic*; here, I think

And, even more insidious, the Deep Ones exist in vast numbers, dispersed across the entirety of the globe, ensconced within vast, watery abysses everywhere — they number (and breed) like *immigrants*.[71] Within the species-being of the Deep Ones we find the perfect synthesis of the sublime and the grotesque (infinite in number, vast in expanse) and the monster as race conspirator. Now we can understand the full implication of the narrator's half-despairing, half-exultant cry, "*No, I shall not shoot myself — I cannot be made to shoot myself!*" He has simply made the move from Kant to Schopenhauer. And, in so doing, he has migrated from the pole of the daemonic to that of the divine. To repeat Otto's comment on this matter: "'Love,' says one of the mystics, 'is nothing else than quenched wrath.'" [72]

We can also immediately partake of this cognizance of Ideas on higher levels, which we receive only by way of external mediation in painting, through purely contemplative perception of plants and observation of animals, and in particular of the latter in their free, natural, and easy state. Objective contemplation of their manifold, wondrous forms and of their doings is an instructive lesson from the great book of nature, is the deciphering of its true "signature of things": we see in it the multiple degrees and manners of manifestation of the will that, one and the same in all beings, wills everywhere the same thing, that is objectified precisely as life, as existence, in such endless variation, such diversity of forms, all of which are accommodations to a diversity of external conditions, comparable to numerous variations on the same

---

he means post-Darwin, as with Ernst Haeckel] evolutionary theory made possible between the individual gestation in the amniotic sac and the evolutionary origin of life from the sea, instantiating in the very body of his narrator the inextricable ties between the individually human and universally organic forces of survival, sexuality, reproduction, and even death." Lovett-Graff, "Shadows over Lovecraft," 187. We all know that Freud stole from Schopenhauer; it would be nice to think that Darwin did the same.

71 Lovett-Graff, "Shadows over Lovecraft," 184.
72 Otto, *The Idea of the Holy*, 24.

thing. But were we to communicate for the sake of the observer's reflection, and in a single word, an insight into that nature's inner essence, then we could best employ for that purpose the Sanskrit formula that appears so often in the holy books of the Hindus and is called *Mahavakya,* i.e., great word: *Tat twam asi.* Which means: "This living thing is you."[73]

The narrator does not scream because he has come to realize that the *grottesche* is the true, and nameless, ground of Being.

---

73 Schopenhauer, *The World as Will and Representation,* 266. Which is, of course, Hegel's definition of Hell: "the Indian knows no reconciliation and identity with Brahman in the sense of the human spirit's reaching *knowledge* of this unity; on the contrary, the unity consists for the Indian precisely in the fact that consciousness and self-consciousness and therefore all the content of the world and the inner worth of man's own personality totally disappears." Hegel, *Aesthetics,* 335.

Conclusion:
The Doom that Came to Humanism

> Nor is it thought that man is either the oldest or the last of earth's masters, or that the common bulk of life and substance walks alone. The Old Ones were, the Old Ones are, and the Old Ones shall be. Not in the spaces we know, but between them, they walk serene and primal, undimensioned and to us unseen.
> — H.P. Lovecraft

> Real power begins where secrecy begins.
> — Hannah Arendt

> What has become unraveled since Dallas is not the plot, of course, not the dense mass of character and events, but the sense of a coherent reality.
> — Don DeLillo

The singularity of Lovecraft's literary achievement is as simple in design as it is daemonic in intent: the single-minded reification of the abject through utilizing the motifs of the weird tale to stage an unspeakable encounter between the rational self and the Wholly Other, culminating in a primal scream that is in equal parts ontological and epistemological. Unfortunately, however, after the scream nothing more can be said, as the presence of the scream is the absence of the very grounds of the possibility of being-human-within-the-world — which would necessarily preclude the possibility of any future writing. Hence Lovecraft's central aesthetic dilemma: is an artistically truthful representation of the world possible if it has been scientifically proven that the universe is meaningless? If, to paraphrase Nietzsche, "there is no Cosmos, only Chaos," is not the anthropocentric discursive framework of humanism rendered permanently irretrievable? Viewed in parapolitical terms — the central concern of this text — the Lovecraftian scream is the "vocalization" of the existential terror of the (eternal) suspension of the false-consciousness of liberalism. And the final, fatal question: after Lovecraft is it possible to continue to conceptualize the state as a specifically *liberal* entity, as liberalism is the classic expression of humanist realism applied to the *ratio* of political speech?

What both Eugene Thacker[1] and Graham Harman[2] have shown in their recent works on Lovecraft, albeit in slightly different ways, is that there is no artistic reason, other than personal preference, for Lovecraft to have written the weird tale. His signature literary effect of discursively migrating between oblique re-presentation and sublimity of substance is, in principle, exportable to virtually any literary genre. The implicit, or even "unconscious" political dimensions of the Mythos have been usefully treated by Thacker in his interesting work *In the Dust of This Planet* (2010). Broadly operating within the current philosophical school of speculative realism, which seeks to problematize both the "object" and the "event" as the central pillars of a post-humanist phenomenology,[3] Thacker opines that the world "is increasingly unthinkable […]. To confront this idea is to confront an absolute limit to our ability to adequately understand the world at all — an idea that has been a central motif of the horror genre for some time."[4] It is this crypto-Lovecraftian "unthinkable world"[5] that forms the key issue for

1 Thacker, *In the Dust of This Planet*.
2 Harman, *Weird Realism*.
3 That is, the subject–self is ontologically subordinate to the object–thing. As in Lovecraft's fiction, the protagonists of speculative realist writing are always phenomena.
4 Thacker, *In the Dust of This Planet*, 1.
5 Ibid.

Thacker: we "cannot help but to think of the world as a human world, by virtue of the fact that it is we human beings that think it."[6] Yet, the sublime nature of increasingly imminent "planetary disasters" (climate change, global extinction[7]) creates a parallel *horror of philosophy,* "the thought of the unthinkable that philosophy cannot pronounce [for to do so would be tantamount to philosophy un-saying itself] but via a non-philosophical language."[8] To paraphrase the good burghers of Munich, when we can no longer have religion (or philosophy, or even science), we can still have art. And the form of art that is most germane to a horror of philosophy is the weird tale; the genre of "supernatural horror is a privileged site in which this paradoxical thought of the unthinkable takes place. What an earlier era would have described through the language of darkness, mysticism or negative theology, our contemporary era thinks of in terms of supernatural horror."[9] Lovecraft, through his deployment of the abject in the service of the weird tale of the un-human provides the aesthetic key for a new and contemporary form of literature: the assaying of *the-world-without-us,* that nebulous and liminal concept that lies between the everyday and common-sense anthropocentric world-for-us and the un-human, world-in-itself, that which is the indescribable signifier of absolute cosmic disinterestism. Poetics becomes indispensable at precisely this point, as Schopenhauer realized, because it is only through signification, metaphor, analogy, and allegory that the inconceivably sublime can be conveyed into a human (albeit non-linear) pattern of meaning; such a thing as the-world-without-us ("nothingness" for Schopenhauer) "should not really be called cognizance, because it no longer has the form of subject and object [nothingness being relative to an existent which is now absent], and is in any case available only to one's own, not further communicable, experience."[10] Horror, therefore, "is about

6   Ibid.
7   For Thacker on extinction, including that of *Homo sapiens,* see ibid., 120–26.
8   Ibid., 2.
9   Ibid.
10 Schopenhauer, *The World as Will and Representation,* 476.

the paradoxical thought of the unthinkable" — the abolition of the possibility of being-human.[11]

What I find most useful in Thacker's account is his discussion of the notion of paradox, which, when

> pursued for the sake of wordless truths [...] can rend veils and even, like the grotesque, approach the holy." Because it breaks the rules, paradox can penetrate to new and unexpected realms of experience, discovering relationships syntax generally obscures. This sense of revelation accompanying a sudden enrichment of our symbolic repertory accounts for our experience of depth: it is very nearly synonymous with *profound*. But while we are in the paradox, before we have either dismissed it as meaningless or broken through to that wordless knowledge (which the meaninglessness of the grotesque image parodies), we are ourselves in "para," on the margin itself.[12]

With this caveat in mind, I would argue that the proper aesthetic question to ask is not whether Lovecraft's writing is good or bad, but whether it is *appropriate*: whether authentic self-knowledge as the necessary prelude to irreparable psychic disintegration may also be artistically appropriated to serve as an aesthetic treatment of a complementary *political disintegration*. It is not without significance that "para," the root of paradox, is also the pre-fix to para-political, classes of political phenomena that may be translated into the literary terms of both the grotesque and the holy — or, at least, the darkly numinous.

Thacker's own thinking on the political implications of theworld-without-us broadly correspond to my own: "Arguably, one of the greatest challenges that philosophy faces today lies in comprehending the world in which we live as both a human *and* a non-human world — and of comprehending this politically."[13]

---

11 Thacker, *In the Dust of This Planet*, 9.
12 Harpham, *On the Grotesque*, 20.
13 Thacker, *In the Dust of This Planet*, 2.

The basis for any sort of manifesto of parapolitical literature would be the revisiting of the foundational principles of classical *occult philosophy*, the uncovering of a local or particular truth that signifies an encompassing unknown world that remains hidden throughout the disquisition.

> This idea — of the occulted world which both makes its presence known and that in doing so reveals to us the unknown — this idea is the dark underside of occult philosophy and its humanist claims [*esoterica* = enlightenment; empowerment]. Against the humanist world-for-us, a human-centric world made in our image, there is the notion of the world as occulted, not in a relative but in an absolute sense. Etymologically speaking, that which is "occult" (*occultus; occulere*) is something hidden, concealed, and surrounded by shadows. However, that which is hidden implies that which is revealed (*revelare*), just as that which is already apparent may, by some twist, suddenly become obscure and occult.[14]

"Occulted" possesses two meanings. The banal one is the *jouissance* of secrecy, and is wholly social in nature.

> That which is occulted can be hidden in a number of ways: something can intentionally be hidden, as when a precious object or important piece of information is stored away or withheld (buried treasure or best-kept secrets). In this case we enter the human world of hide-and-seek, of giving and withholding, of all the micro-exchanges of power that constitute human social networks. We as human beings actively hide and reveal things that, by virtue of this hiding and revealing activity, obtain a certain value for us as knowledge.[15]

The second, and more profound sense is the ontological, the world-without-us.

14 Ibid., 52.
15 Ibid.

> This second type of hiddenness — which may be cataclysmic or everyday — is the hiddenness of the world that we find ourselves thrown into, a hidden world which, regardless of how much knowledge we produce about it, always retains some remainder that lies beyond the scope of our capacity to reveal its hiddenness. In some cases the hidden world is simply the world that does not bend to our will or to our desires, the differential between the world as the world-for-us and the world as the world-in-itself [*cosmic disinterestism*]. In other cases the hidden world may be something like the "unsolved mysteries" that percolate in our popular culture fascination of [*sic*] the paranormal.[16]

Parapolitics, as I have defined it, clearly unifies both senses of Thacker's "hiddenness of the world." Parapolitical realities, precisely because they are in some sense "formless" or "unbounded," correspond perfectly to the literary tropes of the sublime and the grotesque. Yet, precisely because the liminally macroscopic networks of covert agency supersede the conventional anthropocentric reference points of community and state, the parapolitically embedded human subject is effectively reduced to the condition of the abject, at least in terms of orthodox liberal humanism. The Dual/Deep State is the politically unnameable not because it hides so much but because its borders are unknown — and unknowable. It is literally "no-thing" that cannot be situated within any orthodox set of political philosophy.

> When the world-in-itself becomes occulted, or "hidden," a strange and paradoxical movement takes place whereby the world-in-itself presents itself to us, but without ever becoming fully accessible or completely knowable. The world-in-itself presents itself to us, but without simply becoming the world-for-us; it is, to borrow from Schopenhauer, "the world-in-itself-for-us."[17]

16 Ibid., 53.
17 Ibid.

The four signs of the parapolitical (the occluded microscopic revelations which points to the macroscopic hiddenness) — governance, duality, nomadicism, the irrational[18] — are the manifestations of a politics-without-form, which is the Deep State's version of the world-without-us. Not the quantum of its occlusion but the sublimity of its hyper-extension renders the Deep State *monstrum*. Therefore, horror fiction — "a *non-philosophical attempt to think about the world-without-us philosophically*"[19] — ideally lends itself to parapolitical uses. The problem now becomes — exactly how do we make this jump from the weird tale to a specifically parapolitical form of writing?

As the great idiot-savant of horror fiction himself, Stephen King, memorably put it in his pseudo-"reflective" work *Danse Macabre*:

> Terror — what Hunter S. Thompson calls "fear and loathing"[20] — often arises from a pervasive sense of disestablishment: that things are in the un-making. If that sense of unmaking is sudden and seems personal — if it hits you around the heart — then it lodges in the memory as a complete set. Just the fact that almost everyone remembers where he/she was at the instant he/she heard the news of the Kennedy assassination is something almost as interesting as the fact that one nerd with a mail-order gun was able to change the entire course of world history in just fourteen seconds or so.[21]

King's reference to both Oswald and the assassination of JFK is instructive and I will return to it later. For the moment, I want to un-package and render more explicit that which King only elliptically hints at: a natural aesthetic convergence between the

---

18 See above.
19 Thacker, *In the Dust of This Planet*, 9.
20 A really hip variation of Lovecraft's terror and the abject.
21 King, *Danse Macabre*, 8.

horror novel and crime fiction, both of which are in some sense twinned with conspiracy theory. Throughout this text, I have made frequent reference to the strong literary similitudes between the protagonist of the horror story and the much wider-ranging cultural archetype of the detective. In one sense, this relationship is wholly obvious as ratiocination or the uncovering and identification of the Monster serve as one of the main seductions of the horror genre.[22] But on a deeper level, supernatural literature replicates the central ontological premise of all detective fiction: the reestablishment of orthodox cultural and social categories of meaning.[23] The strongest treatment of this theme of ratiocination as metaphysical thriller, from the perspective of detective fiction, is the one presented by Nicole Rafter in her seminal *Shots in the Mirror: Crime Films and Society*. The basic pattern of the detective film is the *search*.

> These tales have [...] "goal-oriented plots," patterns of action to which investigation is key. Mysteries and detective films often mete out clues in small, progressive portions, so that the viewer's process of discovery parallels the investigators. [...] Sometimes [...] they conceal the object of the search, such as the villain's identity, as long as possible. [...] At other

---

22 Carroll, *The Philosophy of Horror*, 178–95. Which obviously links it with horror, at least thematically: "The play of discovery and confirmation, supported by ratiocination, can be found in detective thrillers." Ibid., 186.

23 Care must be taken to observe a clear distinction between the two dominant genres of detective fiction, the classical "who-done-it" and the more contemporary "hard-boiled." Literary criticism ordinarily subsumes the whole of detective literature under the former category, relegating hard-boiled to a sort of grotesque hybrid of the detective and the crime novel. The primary differences between classical and hard-boiled can be largely explained through their respective literary landscapes: who-done-it is English while hard-boiled is American, each genre reflecting the social consciousness of their respective national cultures — social harmony versus alienated individualism. What unites them, however, and which serves as my justification for treating the genre as homogenous, is the dramatic centrality of the figure of the detective whose signature trait is ratiocination. See Grella, "The Formal Detective Novel" and "The Hard-Boiled Detective Novel."

times the goal of the search is clear from the start, and the investigator's job is to find the thing that is missing.²⁴

Detective fiction strictly adheres to a realist epistemology (and ontology) premised upon the intensely optimistic representational theory of language; the final solution of the problem is the establishment of the correct correlation between word and thing. The detective reassures us of "a benevolent and knowable universe [...,] a world that can be interpreted by human reason, embodied in the superior intellect of the detective."²⁵ The detective employs a "practical semiotics," his goal "to consider data of all kinds as potential signifiers and to link them, however disparate and incoherent they seem, to a coherent set of signifieds, that is, to turn them into signs of the hidden *order* behind the manifest conclusion, of the *solution* to the mystery, of the *truth*."²⁶ Therefore, as the successful art of detection is nothing else than the metaphysical validation of the rationality of the cosmos acted out through dramatic means, the function of "the detective hero is to guarantee the readers' absolution from guilt. This is basic to the genre's form of wish fulfilment [...]. What matters is the detective's revelation, not the murders' punishment, for in this myth of rationality truth takes priority over justice."²⁷ As I have already argued in Chapter Three, the detective, as the "twin" of the conspiracy theorist, is a harbinger of modernity. Ratiocination is the hallmark of the detective, the investigator of secret truths who re-arranges reality into the semblance of order; ergo, the sleuth, as well as the conspiracy theorist, is a supremely Cartesian being. Here, I define "Cartesian being" as the personification of the "framework of modernity," identified by Stephen Toulmin as the legacy of the Cartesian Revolution (1618–55).²⁸ Both secular humanism and liberalism

24 Rafter, *Shots in the Mirror*, 190.
25 Grella, "The Formal Detective Novel," 101.
26 Stowe, "From Semiotics to Hermeneutics," 367–68. Emphases in the original.
27 Hilfer, *The Crime Novel*, 2–3 and 4.
28 Toulmin, *COSMOPOLIS*, 98 and 108.

are specifically bourgeois variants of modernity, the "evolution of a new [post-medieval] Cosmopolis, in which the divinely created Order of Nature and the humanly created Order of Society were once again seen as illuminating each other" following the genocidal sectarianism of the Thirty Years War (1618–48).[29] The phrase "illuminating each other" is directly evocative of Heidegger's triptych of *ratio, reor,* and *veritas,* which is only appropriate; as Heidegger's sometime accomplice Carl Schmitt famously argued, metaphysics "is the most intensive and the clearest expression of an epoch."[30] For Schmitt, the "metaphysical image that a definite epoch forges of the world has the same structure as what the world immediately understands to be appropriate as a form of political organization."[31] Accordingly, the "chief girder" of the framework of modernity "to which all the other parts were connected" was the *Cartesian dichotomy*; the "more the extent to which natural phenomena were explained in mechanical terms, as produced by cosmic clockwork, the more (by contrast) the affairs of humanity were allotted to a distinct sphere."[32] The master trope of the Cartesian dichotomy

> was taken to justify a dozen further dichotomies. To summarize: human actions and experiences were *mental* or spontaneous outcomes of reasoning; they were performed, willingly and creatively; and they were active and productive. Physical phenomena and natural processes, by contrast, involved brute matter and were *material*: they were mechanical, repetitive, predictable effects of causes; they merely happened; and matter in itself was passive and inert. Thus the contrast between reasons and causes turned into an outright divorce, and other dichotomies — mental vs. material, actions vs. phenomena, performances vs. happenings, thoughts vs. ob-

---

29 Ibid., 98.
30 Schmitt, *Political Theology*, 46.
31 Ibid.
32 Toulmin, *COSMOPOLIS*, 108.

jects, voluntary vs. mechanical, active vs. passive, creative vs. repetitive — followed easily enough.[33]

As Georges Bataille, a great connoisseur of both the horrific and the abject, declared, "human knowledge becomes the calculation of possibility when it orders the totality of things for itself, the calculation of possibility seized as a foundation."[34] The Cartesian dichotomy is premised upon a separation of Being into two parallel but *non-interactive* domains: nature and humanity, each consisting of its own series of localized antinomies.[35] Nature is governed by fixed laws established during Creation; the objects of physical nature are composed of inert matter; at Creation, Providence arranged natural objects into stable and hierarchical systems of "higher" and "lower" things ("The Great Chain of Being"); as with social "action," natural "motion" flows downwards, from the "higher" creatures towards the "lower" ones.[36] Rational thought and action is the unique signifier of "the human"; rationality (human) and causality (nature) follow different rules, but since thought and action are not governed by natural causality, human actions cannot be explained by strictly scientific means, which yields us the somewhat messy residue of "freedom." Human beings can establish stable systems in society, analogous to the physical systems of nature. As a result, men live "mixed lives," partly rational, partly causal; "as creatures of

33 Ibid. Toulmin's account may be the basis for Thacker's similar estimation: "The human is always relating either to itself or the world. And these two types of relations overlap with each other: the human can only understand the human by transforming it into an object to relate to (psychology, sociology), while the human can only relate to the objective world itself by transforming the world into something familiar, accessible, or intuited in human terms (biology, geology, cosmology)." Thacker, *In the Dust of This Planet*, 30.
34 Bataille, *The Unfinished System of Nonknowledge*, 222.
35 Toulmin, *COSMOPOLIS*, 109–15.
36 This is clearly reminiscent of Schmitt: "All significant concepts of the modern theory of the state are secularized theological concepts not only because of their historical development — in which they were transferred from theology to the theory of the state, whereby, for example, the omnipotent God became the omnipotent lawgiver — but also because of their systematic structure." Schmitt, *Political Theology*, 36.

Reason [i.e., the high], their lives are intellectual or spiritual, as creatures of Emotion [i.e., the low], they are bodily or carnal." The hierarchical subordination of emotion/body to reason/freedom is the capstone of Cartesian ontology.

> Emotion typically frustrates and distorts the work of Reason; so the human reason is to be trusted and encouraged, while the emotions are to be distrusted and restrained [...]. Nature presumably developed as a result of causal, material or mechanical processes: human history was a record of the practical aims, moral decisions and rational methods of human agents. The rational history of humanity and the causal history of nature thus remained, in crucial respects, distinct topics of inquiry until well into the 20th century.[37]

In holding that the "essence of Humanity is the capacity for rational thought and action," Cartesianism implies that all rational deliberation — the totality of "logical operations" performed upon sensory data — takes place within "an 'un-extended' [non-corporeal] realm of thought, locally associated with, but not causally dependent on, physiological mechanisms in the brain."[38] Modernity's universalization of Cartesian rationalism yields a *political ontology* characterized by Schmitt as one of absolute transparency and equivalence: "[T]he democratic thesis of the identity of the ruler and the ruled, the organic theory of the state with the identity of the state and sovereignty [...] the identity of sovereignty and the legal order [...] the identity of the state and the legal order."[39] In this regard, the statist dimension of the Cartesian framework represents the culmination of the onto-political project of the earlier Renaissance with the deployment of linear perspective as a paradigm for good governance.

---

37 Toulmin, *COSMOPOLIS*, 111.
38 Ibid., 113.
39 Schmitt, *Political Theology*, 50.

Painting won its noble imprimatur, was ranked as a fine art, and was awarded almost princely privileges during the Quattrocento. In the centuries that followed it contributed its share toward realizing the metaphysical and political programme of visual and social order. Optical geometry, the ordering of colors and values according to a hierarchy of Neoplatonic inspiration, and the pictorial rules that captured and crystallized the heydays of religious or historical legend helped instill a sense of identity in the new political communities — the City, the State, the Nation — by allotting them the fate of seeing all through reason and thus making the world transparent (clear and distinct). The narrative, urban, architectural, religious and ethical components of these communities were given order on the pictorial plane by the painter's eye, [...] *costruzione legittima* (broadly, the laws of perspective). In turn, the eye of the monarch registered a well-ordered universe all the way to the vanishing point. Exhibited in the churches and the great halls of seigniorial or civic palaces, these representations allowed every member of the community the same possibility as the monarch or the painter for an identity within and mastery over that universe.[40]

In 15th-century Venice, for example, "the ducal procession was the constitution,"[41] whereas in Florence public processions "were used after aborted conspiracies and when illegitimate governments were toppled."[42] In both city-states the onto-political principle was the same: the legitimacy (*legittima*) of *Il Stato* was inseparable from both its capacity to see and to be seen.

> The modern concept of the state — the republic or the democracy — is foreshadowed by this commoner, who in perceptual union with the monarch is a "virtual prince" and

---

40 Lyotard, "Presenting the Unpresentable," 130.
41 Muir, *Civic Ritual in Renaissance Venice*, 190.
42 Trexler, *Public Life in Renaissance Florence*, 337.

> who will later become the citizen. The modern concept of culture stems from this public access to historical-political identifying signs arid to their collective interpretation. Museums perpetuate this tradition; but more pointedly, a glance into the halls of Congress in Washington or into the Chambres des deputes in Paris, attests to the fact that this classical spatial organization is not limited to museum paintings, but structures the representation of the body politic itself.[43]

Rational thought and human freedom are the repository of all forms of value and agency, tantamount to the ontological real and the moral good. From this, it follows that: (i) everything which is irrational is un-real (and evil); and (ii) that which does not accord with human freedom cannot be considered "rational" (or good).

There is a daemonic fly in the ointment, however.

The literary status of the detective as a Cartesian being is wholly dependent upon the stability of the assumed hierarchical order between reason and emotion, the very demarcation that so much of modern literature seeks to invert, a specifically aesthetic incident within the wider philosophical and scientific subversion of the primacy of soul over body that was pictorially announced with the rise of the *grottesche*. In other words, the repressed double of detective fiction is crime fiction, which is premised in an equally but opposite epistemological manner upon the anti-representational nature of language, the ineradicable arbitrariness of the relationship between word and thing. Rafter has brought out the latent "nebulousness" of the crime film brilliantly which, as genre, encapsulates all other genres in which a tension-laden encounter with a paradoxical meaning is dramatically central.

> Crime films do not constitute a genre (a group of films with similar themes, settings and characters) as Westerns and war films do. Rather, crime films constitute a *category* that

---

43 Lyotard, "Presenting the Unpresentable," 130.

encompasses a number of genres — detective movies, gangster films, cop and prison movies, courtroom dramas, and the many offerings for which there may be no better generic label than, simply, crime stories. Like the terms *dramas* and *romances, crime film* is an umbrella term that covers several smaller and more coherent groups.[44]

Tony Hilfer has explicitly stressed anti-Cartesian epistemological pessimism as the central literary conceit of all forms of crime fiction. *"The central and defining feature of the crime novel [or film] is that in it Self and World, guilt and innocence are problematic* [unknowable?]. The world of the crime novel is *constituted* by what is problematic in it," thereby operating to subvert the Cartesian complacency of the detective novel.[45] In contrast, the metaphysical landscape of the crime novel, no less than that of the horror novel, is a wasteland of collapsed categories, what Hilfer denotes as an "ontologically pathological world."

> In [...] crime novels the everyday world of normal perceptions loses its taken-for-granted secure status. In an ontologically pathological world, those under threat must become phenomenologically hyper-acute. The crime novel presents a phenomenologically upside-down world, inverting or intensifying to the point of breakdown the normative structures of perception so brilliantly analyzed in Maurice Merleau-Ponty's *The Phenomenology of Perception*.[46]

Merleau-Ponty's work suffuses the entirety of Hilfer's analysis of the crime novel, of which two points are most germane to my own text. The first is the conspicuous similarity between the schizophrenic and the protagonist of crime fiction, one who bears an uncanny resemblance to the Lovecraftian un-hero: "ev-

---

44 Rafter, *Shots in the Mirror*, 5. I would also add boxing films to the list, a personal favorite of mine. Martin Scorsese's *Raging Bull* (1980) is an outstanding example.
45 Hilfer, *The Crime Novel*, 2.
46 Ibid., 34.

erything is amazing, absurd, or unreal, because the movement of existence towards things no longer has its energy, because it appears to itself in all its contingency, and because the world is no longer self-evident."[47] The crime protagonist is a radically decentered Self who is forced to inhabit a metaphysical cataclysm; when "life has become de-centered" the subject loses all sense of *reor*, objects becoming both "too short and too wide: the majority of events cease to count for me, whereas the nearest ones consume me. They enshroud me like night, and they rob me of individuality and freedom. I can literally no longer breathe: I am possessed."[48] The second is the radically anti-Cartesian *Existenz* of crime's anti-hero: he or she viscerally embodies the paramount error of classical epistemology, which is to reduce awareness to transparency, a metaphysical fallacy masquerading as an epistemological conceit; the *cogito* "teaches us that the existence of consciousness merges with the consciousness of existing, that there can thus be nothing in it of which it is unaware, [and] that reciprocally, everything that it knows with certainty it finds within itself."[49] The deeper paradox at work here is that the recognized pioneer of detective fiction is also one of the God(-less) fathers of horror fiction: Edgar Allan Poe. Just as with those reversible Monster–Gods who eternally move between cosmogony and chaography, the conveyor of order is the instigator of chaos, once stood on his or her head. It is a matter of no little import that the detective writer, such as Poe, who could move from law to horror effortlessly, does so most commonly through the intermediate medium of crime fiction. We are, then, faced with not one but two sets of doubles, each binary pair playing on a slightly different variant of epistemological uncertainty: detective/crime and crime/horror. The elucidation of the epistemic framework of the "irrational" (or anti-modernity, *pace* Toulmin) necessarily carries with it a subversive political

---

47 Merleau-Ponty, *The Phenomenology of Perception*, 300.
48 Ibid., 299. For an historical materialist account of de-centering that also focuses upon schizophrenia, see Jameson, *Postmodernism*, Chapter One, 1–54.
49 Ibid., 351.

subtext, one that disrupts political reason no less than it does moral, scientific, or aesthetic ratio. Our question now becomes: what would a specifically political form of horror-crime fiction actually look like?

My recent thinking on parapolitics — in part occasioned by my simultaneous return to the writings of Lovecraft — has been very much influenced by the situationist theorist Guy Debord and his notion of the "Society of the Spectacle."[50]

> It is precisely here that we can see the profound truth of the Sicilian Mafia's maxim, so well appreciated throughout Italy: "When you've got money and friends, you can laugh at the law." In the integrated spectacle, *the laws are asleep*; because they were not made for the new production techniques, and because they are evaded in distribution by new types of agreement. What the public thinks, or prefers to think, is of no importance. This is what is hidden by all these opinion polls, elections, modernizing restructurings. No matter who the winners are, the faithful customers *will get the worst of it,* because that is exactly what has been produced for them.[51]

A veritable double of criminal sovereignty, spectacular power constitutes "the autocratic reign of the market economy which had acceded to an irresponsible sovereignty and the totality of new techniques of government which accompanied this reign."[52] The hegemony of the Society of the Spectacle, in turn, is signified by the *integrated spectacle,* the cultural reification of mass media as the sole medium and arbiter of "truth"; the "whole life of those societies in which modern conditions of production prevail presents itself as an immense accumulation of spectacles. All that once was directly lived has become mere

---

50 See Wilson, *The Spectacle of the False Flag.*
51 Debord, *Comments,* 69–70.
52 Ibid., 2.

representation."⁵³ As a result, the overall relationship between the social and the visual is governed by a radical functionality.

> If the spectacle — understood in the limited sense of those "mass media" that are its most stultifying superficial manifestation — seems at times to be invading society in the shape of a mere apparatus, it should be remembered that this apparatus has nothing neutral about it, and that it answers precisely to the needs of the spectacle's internal dynamics. If the social requirements of the age which develops such techniques can be met only through their mediation, if the administration of society and all content between people now depends on the intervention of such "instant" communication, it is because this "communication" is essentially *one-way*; the concentration of the media thus amounts to the monopolization by the administrators of the existing system of the means to pursue their particular form of administration.⁵⁴

Once defined as integrated, the spectacle is understood to be socially (and politically) unifying precisely because "the spectacle is not a collection of images; rather, it is a social relationship among people that is mediated by images."⁵⁵ But the spectacle, while unifying in effect, is totalitarian in nature.

> For what is communicated *are orders*; and with perfect harmony, those who give them are also those who tell us what they think of them. [...] A virtually infinite number of supposed differences within the media thus serve to screen what is in fact the result of a spectacular convergence, pursued with remarkable tenacity. Just as the logic of the commodity reigns over capitalist's competing ambitions, and the logic of war always dominates the frequent modifications in weapon-

---

53 Debord, *Society of the Spectacle*, 12.
54 Ibid., 19–20.
55 Ibid., 12.

ry, so the harsh logic of the spectacle controls the abundant diversity of media extravagances.[56]

The effective collapse of media into spectacular power "means quite simply that the spectacle's domination has succeeded in raising a whole generation molded to its laws."[57] Spectacular government,

> which now possesses all the means necessary to falsify the whole of production and perception, is the absolute master of memories just as it is the unfettered master of plans which will shape the most distant future. It reigns unchecked; it *executes its summary judgments.*[58]

The spectacle, therefore, is mediated through its primal political form, spectacular power, which, not at all coincidentally, is "the historical moment by which we happen to be governed."[59] And, within this unbroken social procession of mediating images dwells the hegemony of the *clandestine*: "At the root of the spectacle lies that oldest of all social divisions of labor, the specialization of *power*."[60] And with this comes the operational hegemony of covert agency: "Secrecy dominates this world, and first and foremost as the secret of domination."[61]

> We should expect, as a logical possibility, that the state's security services intend to use all the advantages they find in the realm of the spectacle, which has indeed been organized with that in mind for some considerable time; on the contrary, it is

---

56 Debord, *Comments*, 6–7.
57 Ibid., 7. The parallels with contemporary social media are obvious and do not require comment.
58 Ibid., 10.
59 Debord, *Society of the Spectacle*, 15.
60 Ibid., 18.
61 Debord, *Comments*, 60.

a difficulty in perceiving this which is astonishing and rings false.⁶²

Accordingly,

[n]etworks of promotion/control slide imperceptibly into networks of surveillance/disinformation. Formerly one only conspired against an established order. Today, *conspiring in its favor* is a new and flourishing profession. Under spectacular domination people conspire to maintain it, and to guarantee what it alone would call its well-being. This conspiracy *is a part* of its very functioning.⁶³

What we are confronted with is nothing less than a *horror sensorium* — not the media of horror but a horrific media-as-the-parapolitical-sublime. Just as for Jameson, postmodernism is nothing other than "the consumption of sheer commodification as a process,"⁶⁴ for Debord spectacular power is nothing other than the wholesale collapse of politics into media. The crypto-Burkean corporeal sensorium is a form of the kinesthetic, "a touching experience of feeling through the eye,"⁶⁵ suggesting a subtle interplay between touching and being touched.

The sensorium refers both to the sensory mechanics of the human body and to the intellectual and cognitive functions connected to it: it's integral to the process of perceiving,

---

62 Ibid., 25. This neatly dovetails with the statement provided by CIA Director Richard Helms to the Church Committee (1975–76), the Senate body investigating the assassination operations (or "wet work") undertaken by the CIA during the 1950s and 60s: "When you establish a clandestine service [like] the Central Intelligence Service, you established [*sic*] something totally different from anything else in the United States government. Whether it's right that you should have it, or wrong that you should have it, it works under different rules […] than any other part of the government." Cited in Talbot, *Brothers*, 112.
63 Debord, *Comments*, 74.
64 Jameson, *Postmodernism*, x.
65 Bruno, *Atlas of Emotion*, 219.

and to processing the gamut of sensory stimuli individuals may experience in order to make sense of the world around them.[66]

In the sensorium we face nothing less than the grotesque hybrid of the spectacle and the abject: "Understood on its own terms, the spectacle proclaims the predominance of appearances and asserts that all human life, which is to say all social life, is mere appearance."[67] Viewed through radical criminological lenses, contemporary onto-politics reveals a perpetual migration between antinomies: the public (political) and the private (covert) forms of power. And it is precisely within this eternally unstable double movement that the clandestine power of the spectacle resides.

Although he is notoriously imprecise concerning the historical evolution of the spectacle, in his *Comments* Debord writes that the society of the spectacle had been in existence for "barely forty years" when he first wrote about in in 1967: this would place its genesis sometime during the 1920s, during which time the intensive colonization of social space by late industrial capitalism would have been completed.[68] Jonathan Crary has offered

---

66 Ndalianis, *The Horror Sensorium*, 1. Jameson makes a similar point when discussing postmodern architecture which, for him, "stands as something like an imperative to grow new organs, to expand our sensorium and our body to some new, yet unimaginable, perhaps ultimately impossible dimensions." The architecture of the 1990s, the time of Jameson's ruminations, suggested "a mutation in built space itself" requiring a traumatic (self-induced?) vivisection of our own "perceptual equipment" to facilitate our adaptation to the inhuman "hyperspace" of the postmodern, an "object unaccompanied as yet [1991] by any equivalent mutation in the subject." Jameson, *Postmodernism*, 38 and 39. Re-reading Jameson's neo-Marxist text for this essay forcibly impressed upon me how, and to just what degree, everything that is valuable in Jameson's account was anticipated by Debord. Debord haunts Jameson's text and at one point the latter, when attempting to come up with a more "precise" nomenclature for our anti-revolutionary times, even suggested "spectacle or image society." Ibid., xviii. Perhaps the term that he was looking for was the "post-society of the sublime spectacle."
67 Debord, *Society of the Spectacle*, 14.
68 Debord, *Comments*, 3.

a fascinating explanation for this startling assertion: 1927 was the year of both the perfection of the television by Vladimir Zworkin and the release of Al Jolson's *The Jazz Singer*, the first film that completely synchronized the cinematic image with recorded sound, an event that signalled not only a new cinematic technique but an unprecedented industrial and financial conglomeration as well, the record industry largely subsidizing Hollywood's transition to "talking" films; "as with television, the nascent institutional and economic infrastructure of the spectacle was set in place."[69] The late 1920s was also the period when both Stalinism and fascism grasped the revolutionary potential of the new media technologies for political propaganda. By sheer coincidence, it was also the time of Lovecraft's sojourn in New York.

In other words: wherever you have the occlusion of spectacular power, you must also have the abject. The parapolitically telling words of Lovecraft bear repeating here. Against the emotional primacy of horror "are discharged all the shafts of a materialistic sophistication which clings to frequently felt emotions and external events, and of a naively insipid idealism which deprecates the aesthetic motive and calls for a didactic literature to 'uplift' the reader towards a suitable degree of smirking optimism."[70]

I would like to conclude my essay by revisiting Stephen King's mercifully brief discursus on the assassination of John F. Kennedy and how it relates to the relevance of a literary fusion of parapolitical scholarship with horror fiction; specifically, how Oswald "was able to change the entire course of world history in just fourteen seconds or so." In a moment of profundity rare for an analytic philosopher, Noel Carroll offers the following observation upon the coincidental re-emergence of the horror film and political trauma in the United States during the 1970s.

---

69 Crary, "Spectacle," 457–58.
70 Lovecraft, "Supernatural," 105.

> Since the horror genre is, in a matter of speaking, founded upon the disturbance of cultural norms, both conceptual and moral, it provides a repertory of symbolism for those times in which the cultural order — albeit at a lower level of generality — has collapsed or is perceived to be in a state of dissolution. [...] As a consequence of the Vietnam War and the parade of disillusionments that followed in its trail, Americans have recently and continuously — often for good reason — been disabused of their Dream. Understandably, commentators have traded on the suggestive verbal substitutability of the *American Dream* with the *American Nightmare*. The sense of paralysis, engendered not only by massive historical shocks, but by an unrelenting inability to come to terms practically with situations, which persistently seem inconceivable and unbelievable, finds a ready, though not a total, analogue in the recurrent psychic demoralization of the fictional victims left dumbfounded by horrific monsters. For better or for worse, Americans have been irreparably shaken by "incredible" events and changes for nearly two decades. And horror has been their genre.[71]

One thing that should be evident by now is that horror, both as phenomenology and as aesthetics, has something to do with a preceding cognitive shock of some kind that is either the cause or effect of a wider collapse of cultural categories. The correlation between horror and trauma is argued most persuasively by Thacker.

> Whereas traditional occult philosophy is a hidden knowledge of the open world, occult philosophy today is an open knowledge of the hiddenness of the world.[72] [...] The hidden world, which reveals nothing other than its hiddenness, is a blank, anonymous world that is indifferent to human knowledge, much less to our all-too-human wants and desires.

---

71 Carroll, *The Philosophy of Horror*, 214.
72 Thacker, *In the Dust of This Planet*, 54.

> Hence the hiddenness of the world, in its anonymity and indifference, is a world for which the idea of theistic providence or the scientific principle of sufficient reason, are both utterly insufficient.[73]

As Thacker knows full well, the occluded world is one not merely of ontological but also of political and social abjection.

> Today, in an era almost schizophrenically poised between religious fanatacisms and a mania for scientific hegemony, all that remains is the hiddenness of the world, its impersonal "resistance" to the human *tout court*. Hence, in traditional occult philosophy knowledge is hidden, whereas in occult philosophy today the world is hidden, and, in the last instance, only knowable in its hiddenness. This implies a third shift: whereas traditional occult philosophy is historically rooted in Renaissance humanism, the new occult philosophy is anti-humanist, having as its method the revealing of the non-human as a limit for thought […].[74]

The conventional, "progressive" secular(-ist) liberal who valorizes the public state — naively understood as the "natural" servant of the liberal conscience — is merely unconsciously replicating, or imitating, the parapolitical logic of the Dual State, this time from the presumably "left" side of the artificially constructed "center." Neither too hot nor too cold but lukewarm, the liberal shall be spewed out by the apocalyptic dynamic of history. This is fully on display in the most recent "magisterial" work on Dealey Plaza, *JFK and the Unspeakable: Why He Died & Why It Matters* (2009), by James W. Douglass. The essence of this truly grandiose work on political conspiracy is that the four outstanding political murders in the U.S. during the 1960s (John F. Kennedy, Robert F. Kennedy, Martin Luther King, and Malcolm X) all constitute examples of what Thomas Merton called "the Un-

---

73 Ibid., 53–54.
74 Ibid., 54–55.

speakable": the nihilistic logic and rhetoric of post-Eichmann bureaucratic rationality that underpins a parallel system of clandestine agencies that periodically interfere with the progressive unfolding of social justice. In Douglass's own words:

> Eventually I came to see all four of them together as four versions of the same story. JFK, Malcom, Martin, and RFK were four proponents of change who were murdered by shadowy intelligence agencies using intermediaries and scapegoats under the cover of "plausible deniability." Beneath their assassinations lay the evil void of responsibility that Merton defined as the unspeakable.[75]

In fact, Douglass's entire oeuvre may be usefully understood as an extended exegesis upon Merton's meditations on "the Unspeakable," a phrase that Merton coined while contemplating the "banality" of the evil of Adolf Eichmann.

> *The Unspeakable.* What is this? Surely, an eschatological image. It is the void that we encounter, you and I, underlying the announced programs, the good intentions, the unexampled and universal aspirations for the best of all possible worlds. It is the void that contradicts everything that is spoken even before the words are said; the void that gets into the language of public and official declarations at the very moment when they are pronounced, and makes them ring dead with the hollowness of the abyss. It is the void out of which Eichmann drew the punctilious exactitude of his obedience. […] It is the emptiness of "the end." [76]

If we were to follow Douglass and agree to view JFK's death as the parapolitical will of "the Unspeakable" — itself a neat Lovecraftian turn of phrase — then we would understand that the true nature of the conspiracy theorist's lament over Dallas is

---

75 Douglass, *JFK*, xvii.
76 Merton, *Raids on the Unspeakable*, 4–5.

not "It couldn't have happened by chance," but rather "It was the moment when everything began to go wrong." As Jefferson Morley has perceptively remarked,

> How we make sense of the assassination of John F. Kennedy is directly related to how we make sense of American public life [...]. The events of Nov. 22, 1963, have thus become a kind of national Rorschach test of the American political psyche. Those six seconds of gunfire in Dallas' Dealey Plaza serve as an enigmatic inkblot into which we read our political concerns.[77]

But notice the trap (and the unconscious political conceit of liberalism) laying here: proving that Dallas was a coup d'état will revitalize the anthropocentric strategy of reclaiming history: as what is made by man can be un-made by man, both the coup and its effects can be reversed and history can be saved through a collective act of human will — that is, reason and freedom. Much of the discursive framework of the JFK assassination as a "conspiracy" is premised, implicitly or explicitly, upon another — thoroughly hackneyed — discursive structure widespread throughout the conspiracy community known as "State Crimes Against Democracy" (or SCAD). Broadly situated within the civil libertarian tradition (a phenomenon largely unique to American political culture), SCAD relies upon both an essentialist and an a-historically naïve view of the U.S. Constitution. Its premises include, but are not restricted to: that the Jeffersonian interpretation of the Constitution is the historically correct one; that all of the original Articles concerning the separation of powers and checks and balances must be interpreted literally; that a liberal form of government (the Public State) is both morally optimal and practically achievable; that the U.S. once enjoyed such a system of governance but that it has been under assault from within by "anti-democratic" forces (the Deep State); that this dysfunctional trend has been under way since the creation

---

77 Jefferson Morley in Stone and Sklar, *JFK*, 231.

of the National Security State by Harry Truman in 1947; and that it is the normative imperative of the self-proclaimed "dissident scholar" to reverse these trends. Within this discursive complex, the political murder that took place in Texas assumes a world-historical significance not dissimilar to that of the Holy Grail. From this it follows that the un-covering of the "truth" of Dallas will constitute a politically restorative event (not unlike Kant's subordination of the sublime to the concept) in which the irrational forces of a "false" (un-American?) history will be subdued and the true and proper course of the American experience (the democratic, transparent, and egalitarian Public State) may be reclaimed. In essence, SCAD is nothing less than the naïve reinstatement of the Cartesian dichotomy between nature and humanity wholesale.

"Smirking optimism" with a vengeance.

The ultimate, and most "spectacular," purveyor of this secularist creed is the neo-adolescent crypto-Wagnerian filmmaker Oliver Stone[78]; in his masterpiece of disinformation-with-a-good-conscience, *JFK* (1991), the assassination is relentlessly forced upon the hapless audience as a coup d'état that acts as the signifier of a traumatic but ultimately "containable" historical event: November 22, 1963[79] was the *precise moment* of the usurpation of the public/democratic state by the "shadow government" of the military industrial complex. Very much the narcissistic child of the 1960s and a Vietnam War veteran, the personal trauma undergone by Stone while in Vietnam is clearly but self-servingly repeated by Jim Garrison (Kevin Costner) in a scene that was mercifully deleted from the theatrical release.

> JIM: Just think… just think. What happened to our country… to the world… because of that murder… Vietnam, racial

---

78 Wilson, *The Spectacle of the False Flag*, 264–88.
79 Or 11/22/63, as it is denoted by Stephen King in his monumentally time-wasting eponymous novel.

conflict, breakdown of law, drugs, thought control, assassinations, secret government, fear of the frontier...[80]

In other words — Oliver Stone sounds just like Stephen King.

To be the stone in Stone's shoe: although different surveys yield slightly different results, in general it is a fair estimate that up to 70% of Americans believe that "they have not been told the truth about Dallas." Although it does not logically follow that the majority of this 70% positively believe in a "conspiracy," these (fairly) regular results clearly indicate a basic, though perhaps inarticulate, scepticism concerning the official report prepared by the Warren Commission — and, by extension, of the "truthfulness" of the U.S. government regarding Dallas. So, it would appear that the primary objective of the JFK conspiracy community has been achieved: the majority of Americans doubt the Warren Report. So where, then, lies the revolutionary transformation[81] to be delivered through the revelation of the Truth? In the anti-Cartesian and post-humanist reality of the parapolitical world-without-us, is it even possible to conceive of the "recovery of History"? Or must we be content with our Lovecraftian *jouissance* and maliciously play games with an alternative poetics of a darkly numinous kind?

A parapolitical form of literature utilizing the genre of both crime and horror fiction would be centred upon an unsettling of history as a coherent reality — man is the hapless play-thing not of many-tentacled cosmic entities but nomadic, liminal, and multi-identitied criminogenic forces, either personified or reified. As the proper referent of the form would be the human, the cosmic expanses of the Mythos would have to be excluded, although free use can be made of Jameson's disturbing notions of planetary networks. Similarly, the time dimension would have

---

80 Stone and Sklar, *JFK*, 183.
81 In technical historical parlance, this would be a *reactionary* restorative event, as what is being sought is the return to an earlier state of affairs. In truth, it is the clandestine proliferation of spectacular power that is the truly revolutionary occurrence, a somewhat demoralizing thought for the typical American who can never be anything other than a good liberal.

to be restricted to mere decades — centuries at the most — as the narrative focus would be upon the manifestations(s) of criminal sovereignty and criminogenic asymmetries which would require social being. But the overriding motif will be the *political-world-without-us,* and the most effective means of achieving this vision will be the translation of Schopenhauer's metaphysics into the form of the crime novel. The surest way to accomplish this is to make two highly self-conscious moves in the direction of Schopenhauer's radically post-Kantian (and anti-Hegelian) post-human ontology. The first is to abandon all liberal hope in the salvific properties of history as a purely secular process. The category mistake at the core of the metaphysical system of Hegel is nothing other than the occlusion of history as noumena — self-grounded and radically free — instead of as phenomena — wholly deterministic, inhumanly governed by the categories of time, space, and causality.[82] History as phenomena is chaotic, irrational, contingent, accidental, un-grounded; an "annihilating" determinism that is the ontological foundation of a radically anti-Cartesian epistemology. The parapolitical, by contrast, is analogous to noumena, or the will — absolutely free, out of that extra-judicial boundlessness that enables it to move un-dimensioned between the perceptible planes of political be-

---

82 "Everything of real significance in Kant's project […] comes down to Kant's attempt to 'make room for' the moral life of human beings, to work out some way of defending the possibility of such a free life, while admitting the 'objective reality' of the modern scientific, essentially determinist conception of all nature, including human nature." Pippin, *Hegel's Idealism,* 12. The problem is that you can't; Schopenhauer proved this by reaffirming the unbridgeable abyss between appearance/presentation and reality/will and then reconstituting the latter as the irrational, or contra-rational. I interpret Pippin's work on Hegel's idealism to imply that Hegel attempted to unify noumena with phenomena through the temporal realization of the absolute-as-self-consciousness-and-radical-freedom which is identical with world history. "For Hegel, such a unity [of the whole] could be made out if it could be shown, as he believed he had, that such fundamental human activities were essentially cognitive and that all such attempts at knowledge were, again at some appropriate level, grounded in Absolute subjectivity's attempt at self-knowledge." Ibid., 260. In my opinion, Hegelianism works far better as theology rather than philosophy.

ing while rendered "formless" by that fact alone. Here, I will paraphrase Paul Veyne: History teaches us precisely nothing, for within history one can find examples of absolutely anything. History is literally unbounded, and this extends the inhuman magnitude of the parapolitical to the level of both the sublime-in-the-universal and to the grotesque-in-the-particular, two parallel but equally unlimited "sets" of phenomena. The second is to employ Schopenhauer's anti-Cartesian framework to effect a translation of Otto's *mysterium tremendum* into the discursive terms of a secularized version of conspiracy theory. By "secularized," I mean a conspiratorial text that deploys Lovecraftian motifs but is devoid of the cosmic scale of reference. All of the signature themes of crime writing — the criminality of the everyday (or the "normal"), the multiplicity and duplicity of personal identity, the dissociative nature of the private self, the subversive nature of speech, the internalization of covert strategies of deviance — can, and should, be exploited. But the intended effect should not be the individual concerns ("peasant tragedies"?) of individual transgressions, but the apocalyptic *alētheia* of parapolitical phenomena as the substance of social being. No longer mere crime but a crypto-Debordean *horror sensorium* on a planetary scale.

The hoped-for result will be nothing less than a new hybrid aesthetic of horror and crime.

Weird Noir.

Bibliography

Airaksinen, Timo. *The Philosophy of H.P. Lovecraft: The Route to Horror*. New York: Peter Lang, 1985.

Anderson, Benedict. *Imagined Communities*. London: Verso, 1991.

Arata, Stephen. "'The Occidental Tourist': Dracula and the Anxiety of Reverse Colonization," *Victorian Studies* 33, no. 4. 1990.: 621–45.

Bakhtin, Mikhail. *Rabelais and His World*. Transated by Helene Iswolsky. Bloomington, IN: Indiana University Press, 1984.

Bartelson, Jens. *A Genealogy of Sovereignty*. Cambridge: Cambridge University Press, 1995.

Bataille, Georges. *The Unfinished System of Nonknowledge*, edited by Stuart Kendall, translated by Michelle Kendall and Stuart Kendall. Minneapolis, MN: University of Minnesota Press, 2001.

Beal, Timothy J. *Religion and Its Monsters*. New York: Routledge, 2002.

Bell, Jeffry A. *Philosophy at the Edge of Chaos: Gilles Deleuze and the Philosophy of Difference*. Toronto: University of Toronto Press, 2006.

Berman, Art. *Preface to Modernism*. Chicago: University of Illinois Press, 1994.

Berruti, Massimo. "H.P. Lovecraft and the Anatomy of Nothingness: The Cthulhu Mythos," *Semiotica* 150, no. 1–4. 2004.: 363–418.

Blackwood, Algernon. "The Willows," in *Best Ghost Stories of Algernon Blackwood*, edited by E.F. Bleiler. New York: Dover Publications Inc., 1973.

Bruno, Giuliana. *Atlas of Emotion: Journeys in Art, Architecture, and Film*. New York: Verso, 2002.

Buck-Morss, "Aesthetics and Anaesthetics: Walter Benjamin's Artwork Essay Reconsidered," *October* 62. Autumn 1992.: 3–41.

Budd, Malcolm. *The Aesthetic Appreciation of Nature: Essays on the Aesthetics of Nature*. Oxford: Clarendon Press, 2002.

Burke, Edmund. *A Philosophical Enquiry into the Origin of Our Ideas of the Sublime and Beautiful*. 1759. Menston: The Scolar Press Limited, 1970.

Burleson, Donald R. *Lovecraft: Disturbing the Universe*. Lexington, KY: The University Press of Kentucky, 2009.

Cardin, Matt. *Dark Awakenings*. Poplar Bluff: Mythos Books LLC, 2010.

Carroll, Noel. *The Philosophy of Horror or Paradoxes of the Heart*. New York: Routledge, 1990.

Chambers, R.W. "The Mask." In *The King in Yellow*, 47–68. Suffolk: Dedalus, 1989.

Chesterton, G.K. *The Man Who Was Thursday: A Nightmare*. London: The House of Stratus, 2001.

Clayborough, Arthur. *The Grotesque in English Literature*. Oxford: Clarendon Press, 1965.

Conley, Tom. "Space." In *The Deleuze Dictionary*, edited by Adrien Parr, 257–59. Edinburgh: Edinburgh University Press, 2005.

Crary, Jonathan. "Spectacle, Attention, Counter-Memory." In *Guy Debord and the Situationist International*, edited by Tom McDonough, 455–66. Cambridge: MIT Press, 2002.

Cribb, Robert. "Introduction: Parapolitics, Shadow Governance and Criminal Sovereignty." *Governments of the Shadows: Parapolitics and Criminal Sovereignty*, edited by Eric Wilson, 1–9. London: Plato Press, 2009.

Debord, Guy. *Comments on the Society of the Spectacle*. London: Verso, 1998.

———. *The Society of the Spectacle.* New York: Zone Books, 1995.

Deleuze, Gilles. *Kant's Critical Philosophy,* translated by Hugh Tomlinson and Barbara Habberjam. New York: Continuum, 2008.

——— and Guattari, Félix. *A Thousand Plateaus: Capitalism and Schizophrenia,* translated by Brian Massumi. London: The Athlone Press, 1988.

Derrida, Jacques, *The Truth in Painting,* translated by Geoff Bennington and Ian McLeod. Chicago: University of Chicago Press, 1987.

Douglass, James W. *JFK and the Unspeakable: Why He Died and Why It Matters.* New York: Orbis Books, 2009.

Dziemianowicz, Stefan. "Outsiders and Aliens: The Uses of Isolation in Lovecraft's Fiction." In *An Epicure in the Terrible : A Centennial Anthology of Essays in Honor of H.P. Lovecraft,* edited by David E. Schultz and S.T. Joshi, 165–95. New York: Hippocampus Press, 2011.

Eagleton, Terry. *The Ideology of the Aesthetic.* Oxford: Blackwell, 1998.

Engdahl, William F. *A Century of War: Anglo-American Oil Politics and the New World Order.* London: Pluto Press, 2004.

———. *Full Spectrum Dominance: Totalitarian Democracy in the New World Order.* Edition Engdahl: 2009.

———. *Gods of Money: Wall Street and the Death of the American Century.* Edition Engdahl: 2010.

Geuss, Raymond. *History and Illusion in Politics.* Cambridge: Cambridge University Press, 2001.

Grella, George. "The Formal Detective Novel." In *Detective Fiction: A Collection of Critical Essays,* edited by Robin W. Winks, 84–102. Woodstock: A Foul Play Press Book, 1988.

———. "The Hard-Boiled Detective Novel." In *Detective Fiction: A Collection of Critical Essays,* edited by Robin W. Winks, 103–20. Woodstock: A Foul Play Press Book, 1988.

Griffin, David Ray. *The New Pearl Harbor: Disturbing Questions About the Bush Administration and 9/11.* Northampton: Olive Branch Press, 2004.

——— and Peter Dale Scott, eds. *9/11 and American Empire: Intellectuals Speak Out,* Vol. I. Northampton: Olive Branch Press, 2007.

Hall, Stephen and Simon Winlow, eds. *New Directions in Criminological Theory.* London: Routledge, 2012.

Hanegraaff, Wouter J. "Fiction in the Desert of the Real: Lovecraft's Cthulhu Mythos," *Aries* 7. 2007.: 85–109.

Harms, Daniel, *The Cthulhu Mythos Encyclopedia: A Guide to H.P. Lovecraft's Universe.* Third Edition. Lake Orion: Elders Sign Press, 2008.

Harpham, Geoffrey Galt. *On the Grotesque: Strategies of Contradiction in Art and Literature.* Princeton: Princeton University Press, 1982.

Harman, Graham. *Weird Realism: Lovecraft and Philosophy.* Winchester: Zero Books, 2012.

Heidegger, M. *Identity and Difference.* Translated by Joan Stambaugh. New York: Harper & Row Publishers, 1969.

———. *Parmenides.* Translated by Andre Schuwer and Richard Rojcewicz. Bloomington: Indiana University Press, 1992.

Hegel, G.W.F. *Aesthetics: Lectures on Fine Art.* Vol. I. Translated by T.M. Knox. Oxford: Clarendon Press: 1975.

———. *Introductory Lectures on Aesthetics.* Translated by Bernard Bosanquet. London: Penguin Books, 2004.

Hilfer, Tony. *The Crime Novel: A Deviant Genre.* Austin: University of Texas Press, 1990.

Houellebecq, Michel. *H.P. Lovecraft: Against the World, Against Life.* London: Weidenfeld & Nicolson, 2006.

Israel, Jonathan I. *Radical Enlightenment: Philosophy and the Making of Modernity 1650–1750.* Oxford: Oxford University Press, 2001.

Jameson, Fredric. *The Geopolitical Aesthetic: Cinema and Space in the World System.* Indianapolis: Indiana University Press, 1992.

———. *Postmodernism or, the Cultural Logic of Late Capitalism.* Durham: Duke University Press, 1991.

Joshi, S.T. "Explanatory Notes." In H.P. Lovecraft, *The Call of Cthulhu and Other Weird Stories,* edited by S.T. Joshi, 361–420. London: Penguin Books, 2011.

———. "Explanatory Notes." In H.P. Lovecraft, *The Thing on the Doorstep and Other Weird Stories,* edited by S.T. Joshi, 367–443. London: Penguin Books, 2001.

———. *H.P. Lovecraft: A Life.* West Warick: Necronomicon Press, 1996.

———. *H.P. Lovecraft: The Decline of the West.* Berkeley Heights: Wildside Press, 1990.

———."Introduction," in In H.P. Lovecraft, *The Thing on the Doorstep and Other Weird Stories,* edited by S.T. Joshi, vii–xvi. London: Penguin Books, 2001.

Kant, Immanuel. *The Critique of Judgment,* translated by J. H. Bernard. Amherst: Prometheus Books, 2000.

Kayser, Wolfgang. *The Grotesque in Art and Literature.* New York: Columbia University Press, 1957.

King, Stephen. *Danse Macabre.* Reprint edition. New York: Gallery Books, 2010.

Knox, T.M., Translator's Preface to G.W.F. Hegel, *Aesthetics: Lectures on Fine Art, Volume One,* trans. T.M. Knox, v–xiv. Oxford: Clarendon Press, 1975.

Kristeva, Julia. *Powers of Horror: An Essay on Abjection.* Translated by Leon S. Roudiez. New York: Columbia University Press, 1982.

Levy, Maurice. *Lovecraft: A Study in the Fantastic.* Detroit: Wayne State University, 1988.

Lovecraft, H.P. *At the Mountains of Madness: The Definitive Edition.* New York: The Modern Library, 2005.

———."At the Mountains of Madness." In H.P. Lovecraft, *At the Mountains of Madness: The Definitive Edition,* 1–102. New York: The Modern Library, 2005.

———. "The Call of Cthulhu." In Michel Houellebecq, *H.P. Lovecraft: Against the World, Against Life,* 121–57. London: Weidenfeld & Nicolson, 2006.

———. "The Doom that Came to Sarnath." In H.P. Lovecraft, *The Haunter of the Dark and Other Stories*, edited by M.J. Elliott, 31–7. London: Wordsworth Editions, 1987.

———. "The Dunwich Horror." In H.P. Lovecraft, *The Thing on the Doorstep and Other Weird Stories*, edited by S.T. Joshi, 206–45. London: Penguin Books, 2001.

———. "Facts Concerning the Late Arthur Jermyn and His Family." In H.P. Lovecraft, *The Call of Cthulhu and Other Weird Stories*, edited by S.T. Joshi, 14–23. London: Penguin Books, 2011.

———. *The Haunter of the Dark and Other Stories*, edited by M.J. Elliott. London: Wordsworth Editions, 1987.

———. "He." In H.P. Lovecraft, *The Call of Cthulhu and Other Weird Stories*, edited by S.T. Joshi, 119–29. London: Penguin Books, 2011.

———. *The Call of Cthulhu and Other Weird Stories*, edited by S.T. Joshi. London: Penguin Books, 2011.

———. "The Case of Charles Dexter Ward." In H.P. Lovecraft, *The Thing on the Doorstep and Other Weird Stories*, edited by S.T. Joshi, 90–205. London: Penguin Books, 2001.

———. "The History of the Necronomicon," in Lovecraft, *The Haunter of the Dark,* 311–12. London: Wordsworth Editions, 1987.

———. "The Horror at Red Hook." In H.P. Lovecraft, *The Haunter of the Dark and Other Stories*, edited by M.J. Elliott, 125–46. London: Wordsworth Editions, 1987.

———. "The Music of Erich Zann." In H.P. Lovecraft, *The Thing on the Doorstep and Other Weird Stories*, edited by S.T. Joshi, 45–52. London: Penguin Books, 2001.

———. "The Shadow over Innsmouth." In H.P. Lovecraft, *The Haunter of the Dark and Other Stories*, edited by M.J. Elliott, 329–92. London: Wordsworth Editions, 1987.

———. "Supernatural Horror in Literature." In H.P. Lovecraft, *At the Mountains of Madness: The Definitive Edition*, 103–73. New York: The Modern Library, 2005.

———. *The Thing on the Doorstep and Other Weird Stories*, edited by S.T. Joshi. London: Penguin Books, 2001.

———. "The Tomb." In H.P. Lovecraft, *The Thing on the Doorstep and Other Weird Stories,* edited by S.T. Joshi, 1–10. London: Penguin Books, 2001.

———. "The Unnamable." In H.P. Lovecraft, *The Haunter of the Dark and Other Stories,* edited by M.J. Elliott, 91–98. London: Wordsworth Editions, 1987.

———. "The Whisperer in Darkness." In Michel Houellebecq, *H.P. Lovecraft: Against the World, Against Life,* 159–237. London: Weidenfeld & Nicolson, 2006.

Lovett-Graff, Bennett, "Shadows over Lovecraft: Reactionary Fantasy and Immigrant Eugenics," *Extrapolation* 38, no. 3. 1997.: 175–92.

Lyotard, Jean-François. *Lessons on the Analytic of the Sublime. Kant's "Critique of Judgment," ss. 23–29.,* translated by Elizabeth Rottenberg. Stanford: Stanford University Press, 1994.

———. "Presenting the Unpresentable: The Sublime." In *The Sublime,* edited by Simon Morley, 130–36. Cambridge: MIT Press, 2010.

———."The Sublime and the Avant-Garde." In *The Sublime,* edited by Simon Morley, 27–41. Cambridge: MIT Press, 2010.

MacCormack, Patricia. "Lovecraft Through Deleuzio-Guattarian Gates," *Postmodern Culture* 20, no. 2 (January, 2010). http://muse.jhu.edu.ezproxy.lib.monash.edu.au/journals/postmodern_culture/v20/20...10/03/2013.

Mariconda, Steven J. "Lovecraft's Cosmic Imagery." In *An Epicure in the Terrible: A Centennial Anthology of Essays in Honor of H.P. Lovecraft,* edited by David E. Schultz and S.T. Joshi, 196–207. New York: Hippocampus Press, 2011.

Martin, Sean Elliot. *H.P. Lovecraft and the Modernist Grotesque.* Published by author, 2008.

McDonough, Tom, ed. *Guy Debord and the Situationist International: Texts and Documents.* Cambridge: MIT Press, 2002.

Meikle, Jeffrey L. "'Other Frequencies': The Parallel Worlds of Thomas Pynchon and H.P. Lovecraft," *Modern Fiction Studies* 27, no. 2 (1981): 287–94.

Merleau-Ponty, Maurice. *Phenomenology of Perception.* Translated by Donald A. Landes. London: Routledge, 2012.

Merton, Thomas. *Raids on the Unspeakable*. New York: New Directions, 1964.

Michalowski, Raymond, "Power, Crime and Criminology in the New Imperial Age," *Crime, Law and Social Change* 51. 2009.: 303–25.

Mieville, China. Introduction to H.P. Lovecraft, *At the Mountains of Madness: The Definitive Edition*, xi–xxv. New York: The Modern Library, 2005.

Morley, Jefferson. "The Political Rorschach Test." In Oliver Stone and Zachary Sklar, *JFK: The Book of the Film*, 231–34. New York: Applause Books, 1992.

Morley, Simon. "Introduction: The Contemporary Sublime." In *The Sublime*, edited by Simon Morley, 12–21. Cambridge: MIT Press, 2010.

———, ed. *The Sublime*. Cambridge, MA: MIT Press, 2010.

Muir, Edward. *Civic Ritual in Renaissance Venice*. Princeton: Princeton University Press, 1981.

Ndalianis, Angela. *The Horror Sensorium: Media and the Senses*. Jefferson: McFarland, 2012.

Nisbet, Robert. *The Social Philosophers: Community and Conflict in Western Thought*. London: Heinneman, 1974.

Otto, Rudolf. *The Idea of the Holy: An Inquiry into the Non-Rational Factor in the Idea of the Divine and its Relation to the Rational*. Translated by John W. Harvey. Oxford: Oxford University Press, 1958.

Parr, Adrien, ed. *The Deleuze Dictionary*. Edinburgh: Edinburgh University Press, 2005.

Pippin, Robert B. *Hegel's Idealism: The Satisfactions of Self-Consciousness*. Cambridge: Cambridge University Press, 1989.

Rafter, Nicole. *Shots in the Mirror: Crime Films and Society*. Second edition. Oxford: Oxford University Press, 2006.

Ralickas, Vivian. "'Cosmic Horror' and the Question of the Sublime in Lovecraft," *Journal of the Fantastic in the Arts* 18, no. 3 (2007): 364–98.

Schmitt, Carl. *Political Theology: Four Chapters on the Concept of Theology*. Translated by George Schwab. Chicago: University of Chicago Press, 2005.

Schopenhauer, Arthur. *The World as Will and Representation.* Vol. I. Translated by Richard E. Aquila and David Carus. New York: Pearson/Longman, 2008.

Schultz, David E. "From Microcosm to Macrocosm: The Growth of Lovecraft's Cosmic Vision." In *An Epicure in the Terrible: A Centennial Anthology of Essays in Honor of H.P. Lovecraft,* edited by David Schultz and S.T. Joshi, 208–29. New York: Hippocampus Press, 2011.

——— and Joshi, S.T., eds. *An Epicure in the Terrible: A Centennial Anthology of Essays in Honor of H.P. Lovecraft.* New York: Hippocampus Press, 2011.

Scott, Peter Dale. *American War Machine: Deep Politics, the CIA Global Drug Connection, and the Road to Afghanistan.* New York: Rowman & Littlefield Publishers, Inc., 2010.

———. *Deep Politics and the CIA Global Drug Connection: Heroin and the Networks of Domination.* Private copy. 2009.

———. *Deep Politics and the Death of JFK.* Berkeley: University of California Press, 1993.

———. *Minding the Darkness: A Poem for the Year 2000.* New York: New Directions, 2000.

———. *The Road to 9/11: Wealth, Empire and the Future of America.* Berkeley: University of California Press, 2007.

———. *The War Conspiracy: JFK, 9/11, and the Politics of War.* New York: Mary Ferrell Foundation Press, 2008.

Smith, Daniel W. "Translator's Introduction: Deleuze on Bacon: Three Conceptual Trajectories in The Logic of Sensation." In Gilles Deleuze, *Francis Bacon: The Logic of Sensation,* translated by Daniel W. Smith, vii–xxvii. Minneapolis: University of Minnesota Press, 2003.

Stone, Oliver and Zachary Sklar. *JFK: The Book of the Film.* Research notes compiled by Jane Rusconi. New York: Applause Books, 1992.

Stowe, William W. "From Semiotics to Hermeneutics: Modes of Detection in Doyle and Chandler." In Glen W. Most and William W. Stowe, *The Poetics of Murder: Detective Fiction and Literary Theory,* 366–83. New York: Harcourt Brace Jovanovich, 1983.

Talbot, David. *Brothers: The Hidden History of the Kennedy Years*. London: Pocket Books, 2007.

Thacker, Eugene. *In the Dust of This Planet: Horror of Philosophy*. Vol. 1. Winchester: Zero Books, 2011.

Thomson, Philip. *The Grotesque*. London: Methuen & Co Ltd, 1972.

Toulmin, Stephen. *COSMOPOLIS: The Hidden Agenda of Modernity*. New York: The Free Press, 1990.

Trexler, Richard C. *Public Life in Renaissance Florence*. Ithaca: Cornell University Press, 1980.

Tunander, Ola. "Democratic State vs. Deep State: Approaching the Dual State of the West," In *Government of the Shadows: Parapolitics and Criminal Sovereignty*, edited by Eric Wilson, 56–72. London: Pluto Press, 2009.

Will, Bradley A. "H.P. Lovecraft and the Kantian Sublime," *Extrapolation* 43, no. 1 (2002): 7–21.

Wilson, Eric. "The Concept of the Parapolitical." In *The Dual State: Parapolitics, Carl Schmitt, and the National Security Complex*, edited by Eric Wilson, 1–31. London: Ashgate, 2012.

———. "Crimes Against Reality: Parapolitics, Simulation, and Power Crime." In *New Directions in Criminological Theory*, edited by Stephen Hall and Simon Winlow 292–316. London: Routledge, 2012.

———. "Deconstructing the Shadows." In *Government of the Shadows: Parapolitics and Criminal Sovereignty*, edited by Eric Wilson, 13–55. London: Pluto Press, 2009.

———, ed. *Government of the Shadows: Parapolitics and Criminal Sovereignty*. London: Pluto Press, 2009.

———, ed. *The Dual State: Parapolitics, Carl Schmitt, and the National Security Complex*. London: Ashgate, 2012.

———. *The Savage Republic: De Indis of Hugo Grotius, Republicanism, and Dutch Hegemony in the Early Modern World-System. c. 1600–1619*. Leiden: Martinus Nijhoff, 2008.

———. *The Spectacle of the False Flag: Parapolitics from JFK to Watergate*. Brooklyn: Punctum Books, 2015.

Winks, Robin W., ed. *Detective Fiction: A Collection of Critical Essays*. Woodstock: A Foul Play Press Book, 1988.

Wisnicki, Adrian S. *Conspiracy, Revolution, and Terrorism from Victorian Fiction to the Modern Novel.* New York: Routledge, 2008.

Woodard, Ben. *Slime Dynamics: Generation, Mutation, and the Creep of Life.* Winchester: Zero Books, 2012.